NATIVE AMERICANS:

23 INDIAN BIOGRAPHIES

by

Dr. Roger W. Axford

Published by
The A. G. Halldin Publishing Company
Indiana, Pennsylvania
15701

ISBN 0-935648-02-X

FORWARD

Even more than other minorities, Indians remain a mystery to most Americans. Old images still cloud our vision -- the Noble Savage, the silent, stoical tribal elder, the crafty warrior. More recently, the word "Indian" to most Anglos has come to evoke either alcoholism, high steel work, or Wounded Knee.

These stereotypes arise because of a "knowledge vacuum" that has many roots. In part it is historical: whole tribal societies were eradicated without any attempt at understanding by the dominant culture. In part it is geographic: most reservations are located far from the cities, and every relatively large urban Indian concentrations are tiny in comparison to the size of our cities. And surely there is a large willful element in this ignorance, part of the anti-Indian bigotry that has existed from the days of the earliest white settlers.

But real human understanding is inhibited by both ignorance and sentimentalization. The purpose of this book is to offer insights into Native American life by studying Native American lives -- the stories of 23 individuals and their careers in fields ranging from art and athletics to education and engineering.

Most of these stories are the kind that don't make the history books. Yet they are memorable and important, for they relate the ways in which ordinary people achieve the extraordinary -- making a direct, positive impact on their communities, and enriching not only the lives of their neighbors, but of all of us.

Morris K. Udall,
Member of Congress
(January 1977)

Table of Contents

Dr. Louis W. Ballard

Cherokee and Sioux
MUSICIAN - COMPOSER

Dr. Louis W. Ballard

Dr. Louis W. Ballard learned and absorbed the songs and dances of his Indian people from his earliest childhood. Born in Quapaw, Oklahoma, of Cherokee-Quapaw extraction, he descended from chiefs on both sides of his family.

Dr. Louis W. Ballard is a many talented person. He is a composer, writer, music educator, and a lecturer-clinician on Indian music, and holds workshops throughout the nation.

Dr. Ballard believes in using materials at hand to make music. For example, he used a commode float to make his own metal rattle. Raymond G. Van Diest, Music Consultant for the Arizona Department of Education says of Louis Ballard, who has developed curriculum planning for the Department of Interior, for over 400,000 Indian youth in 276 Bureau of Indian Affairs schools nationwide:

"Dr. Ballard is one of the first American Indians to publish authentic learning materials, representing the Indian peoples of the United States. The importance of the ethnic heritage of the American Indian is emerging more prominently every day."

ACCOMPLISHMENTS

Dr. Ballard won the Indian Achievement Award for 1972, the first musician to receive this distinguished award. He was named Indian of the Year for 1973 by the American Indian Exposition in Anadarko, Oklahoma. He was the recipient of the Annual Ed-Press Award for Educational Journalism for his article, "Put American Indian Music in the Classroom" published in the MUSIC EDUCATIONS JOURNAL.

In addition to his accomplishments in music education, Dr. Ballard is an eminent composer, for his varied works have been preformed by leading American orchestras, bands, chamber ensembles, ballet companies, and leading soloists throughout our western world. His world premier for orchestra was played by the symphony at Phoeniz, Arizona on January 19, 1976. The Phoenix Symphony played his "Incident at Wounded Knee". He was the first recipient of the Marion Nevins MacDowell Award for his woodwind quintet composition.

In 1967, the Phoenix Symphony introduced Dr. Ballard's WHY THE DUCK HAS A SHORT TAIL during a concert tour of the Indian reservations in New Mexico and Arizona. Ray Boley of Canyon Records in Phoenix, produced a multi-media teaching package for this prominant Indian musician. The work titled

AMERICAN INDIAN MUSIC FOR THE CLASSROOM took two years of researching, compiling and editing to develop. Twenty-two (22) Indiana tribes and eight cultural areas of the United States are represented in the four-record cultural musical learning package. There is an 88 page teachers' guide which can be used by universities, Indian Centers, lower schools, museums, libraries, and multi-cultural programs in the U.S. and Canada.

Dr. Ballard has studied privately with eminent musicians Mario Castelnuovo-Tedesco and Darius Milhaud. He is a graduate of Tulsa University in Oklahoma, and the University of Oklahoma.

Dr. Ballard says of the Indian music he has produced:

"It is not enough to acknowledge that American Indian music is different from other music . . . What is needed in America, as it has always been needed, is an awakening and re-orienting or our total spiritual and cultural perspective to embrace, understand, and learn from the aboriginal American what it is that motivates his musical and artistic impulse."

He says that Indian music is different from other music, and that the Indian, somehow, "marches to a different drum." Dr. Ballard feels that "the songs we are bringing into the classroom are readily acceptable to a lot of third-culture peoples, including blacks, Spanish-Americans, Orientals. They all respond to Indian music" he told Jim Newton of the Phoenix-Gazette.

Dr. Ballard is perturbed that even the Indian children do not know their own culture. He says:

"For a long time the white man was trying to make a 'civilized' man of the Indian and 50 years ago there was a cultural genocide policy in which the Indian was told not to speak his language and not to sing his songs."

"This was the policy of the Bureau of Indian Affairs Schools, church schools, and public schools. Now this has changed. Here at last is an opportunity for the Indian to Americanize the white and black children. But even the Indian children don't know their own culture."

Dr. Ballard pointed up that the music he writes spills over into the ecology, since the Indian honored the environment among which he lived. He philosophized:

"Indians learned a great deal from nature, and we've got to preserve these things and not change the natural order of things. He even used drums of animal hides and other musical instruments using natural materials. The duck dance song honors the coming of the ducks for the winter." Ballard brought many of the native instruments he has collected over the many years of working with music, when he did his recordings.

3

Dr. Ballard is the chairman of the Music and Performing Arts Department of the Institute of American Indian Arts in Santa Fe, New Mexico. He has receive an honorary Doctorate of Music degree from the College of Sante Fe. This composer would like to see a symposium on Indian arts, a multimedia presentation that would include music, dance, art. The best possibility appears to be an American Indian opera, possibly based on the life of Will Rogers, who was part Indian, and had many Indian associations. Ballard recalls that "Eskimos sang an Indian dirge as they brought his body from the plane when it crashed in Alaska." Already Dr. Ballard has written a choral cantata, "Portrait of Will," which the Kansas City Symphony premiered with the son, Will Rogers, Jr., as the narrator.

Dr. Ballard is married to Ruth Dore, a concert pianist, who first performed his works in New York. They have three children Anne Marie, Louis Anthony, and Charles Christopher.

Mrs. Ballard feels that Dr. Ballard is helping to overcome racial prejudice. She says: "The way the Indian has to overcome racism is to excell in his chosen field. The Indian artist has to be a greater person, a greater artist than others. This is a tremendous responsibility. There is prejudice, and this is the way to improve the image of the American Indian."*

*Phone Interview, Nov. 11, 1976.

Walter Currie

Canadian Ojibway
PROFESSOR - PHILOSOPHER

Walter Currie

I am a city Indian. I am not a reserve Indian. My childhood knowledge of the Reserve is a recollection of spending holidays there, or visiting relatives.

At the same time, the city where we lived was not so far that our relatives visited us on a regular basis. My parents way of raising me would be classified as permissive. But I would classify it as complete freedom, where I, the child, am expected to accept the responsibility for my actions.

One time my Dad and Mother talked to me. They told me that whatever you do, or wherever you go, don't be ashamed to come home. My father was self-educated, a well-read person, with a sense of humor and musical talent. He played the piano and guitar and sang; he was also a motor mechanic by self-taught skills.

My Mother was illiterate, could neither read nor write English, but was bilingual, perfect in Ojibway. Until the day she died she could not say the beginning "th" sound. With regard to cultural life-style, the sharing concept was quite evident in our home. As soon as company came, Mother would start the fire and start to cook. One time, I remember, our uncle Allen and the family came over from the Island, and just Dad and I were home. Evidently we had nothing in the house, so Dad reached into his pocket and pulled out his only quarter. He said, "Go get five tins of sardines," and we fed our company.

WHAT VALUES DO YOU THINK SHOULD BE SHARED FROM THE INDIAN LIFE-STYLE?"

The standard which one finds in all societies in varying degrees is respect for elders. The Western societies complain that this is disappearing, and yet among native communities, this is to me still quite strong. It is something which children learn without being taught directly. The relationship between children and adults is such that one does not ask or challenge.

I remember a visit to Northern Ontario. The Chief and men sat around the room talking. His eight-year-old son sat at the side and said nothing. But, all at once the child arose, went outside, was gone over half an hour. I noticed no one told him to put on his coat or mittens, and it was forty below. When he returned no one asked him where he had been, or why he was gone so long. It is this kind of responsibility, independence, and trust which I noticed still among Native people even today. It underlines the relationship whereby grown-ups look on children as people, not as young adults, but as people in every aspect. I accept the child as a person for what he is.

Another thing that needs to be put forward is what the elders have known for a long time--it is the recognition that there is a Supreme Spirit, not a Being, but a Spirit; who like Jehovah, has created all that walks, flys, crawls and creeps. This is where we differ from Christianity, in that we are a part of the circle of life. Christians are told in the Old Testament, that Man shall have dominion over and shall subdue the world. Our people have been taught that if you remove the elements from the circle, the man dies. If you remove the insects from the circle, man dies; if you remove the plants from the circle, man dies. But if you remove man from the circle, the circle becomes stronger that man is a brother to all things, and therefore must work to live in harmony with all things.

I would like to think that instead of our being Americans or Canadians, we will be one North Americans, which will reflect a new philosophy in keeping with the New World. We have much to offer if we can really make a reality of a pluralistic society which truly accepts differences.

Democratic education seems to mean the same for everybody, which raises the question, "Who determines what that sameness shall be?" The leveling is often to the lesser value, rather than to a series of values. You can't level education, any more than you can say that any one racial group looks the same, it just isn't true.

One can remain a native person in the dominant society. In the old days, when father hunted, he knew that to kill the deer or moose he had to know all there was to know about the deer or moose. He had to in essence become a deer or moose in order to kill, to put food and clothing in the house for the family. He also knew that he did not have to remain that deer or moose. In the same way today, a native person to survive in the dominant society, has to learn their ways but does not have to become one of them.

There is a warning in there that, as the old people did not remain a deer or moose, they still acquired some aspects of those animals, which were and are considered worthwhile. Similarly, a young person today has the opportunity of choosing those aspects of the dominant society which he or she thinks are worthwhile. Of course that raises the point that Native life-style is that I have no right to criticize you, nor will you criticize me. Instead, I wait for you to prove to me that you are not worthy of my acceptance.

7

Ida Carmen

Mono of California
BASKETMAKER

Ida Carmen

(Cabin three miles up California 222 North Fork, CA Daughter-Viola Magee)

HOW MANY MONO INDIANS ARE STILL LIVING?

I would guess about two hundred and fifty. . .spread out all over California. There are few jobs here so many of the Mono Indians left.

I was born here in North Fork, Madera County, my mother and grandmother were born here. My family made a living fishing and picking acorn and making acorn. We take it out of the Oak tree. It is our main course. We eat it with mushrooms, rabbit, squirrels, deer meat and fish. We gather the acorn in the fall. Sometimes it freezes and we don't get any. We dry it and store it. We grind it.

WHAT KIND OF CRAFTS DO YOU DO?

I make the baby baskets, winnowing baskets, acorn baskets, and some knick-knack baskets. I make sewing baskets made out of red-bud bush. It is a shoot and it grows right back after we cut it. We use the baskets to hold fruit and clean our acorn into it when we crack it.

They have the rock we grind the acorn with in the Sierra Mono Museum, down the road. People come from all over to see the arts and crafts. We had a large crowd of school children from Fresno yesterday. We do our work at the Museum on Thursdays. . .

We have a bake sale and dance and make money for the museum. The museum is entirely private. . . the Mono Indians built it and own it.

We hold an Indian Festival for all the Mono Indians in the second week of August. I have 10 children, five girls and five boys. My husband died two years ago. One daughter lives in Washington and a daughter lives in Salinas, California. My son, Chester, does logging in Eureka. Another son works in construction in Chowchilla (Chowchilla, California). My oldest son, Rayna Tom Carmen, lives here and is retired. . .

WHAT MEMORIES DO YOU HAVE OF YOUR CHILDHOOD?

I didn't have any father. . .my mother had about five children. She did gold mining, picking cotton and picking grapes. They cut

10

wood for people those days. Mostly we lived on the stuff we got around here.

I am eighty-one. I just had a birthday. Some like to sell the acorn biscuits. We call them ikuba. . . the drink is yamina. . . which is made from the acorn. We drink it warm or cold. It is really nourishing. . .

This is our own place. We are fighting for our rights. We never got anything from the Bureau of Indian Affairs. . .we got $600 for our land, that was about eight years ago. We have about one hundred and twenty acres. Welfare told us to give it to the two boys. . .they told me I could live here as long as I am living. . .

We went barefooted and when we were children we walked three miles to school. We didn't go much to school.

ARE YOU TEACHING THE CRAFTS OF BASKETWEAVING TO THE CHILDREN?

They don't want to learn. They are too busy. They go to the cities. As soon as they get out of the school they are out making a living. My children worked in the shipyards in San Francisco during the war. They never learned the crafts. . .there are other Monos in the valley that make baskets.

WHAT HOPES FOR THE INDIAN PEOPLE DO YOU HAVE?

The Indians are trying to get their recognition in the books. The Monos are seldom mentioned. The American people don't know us. They have been having meetings and Governor Edmund Brown was here yesterday.

They said they are going to look into giving some help to the Mono people. They said we are not treaty Indians. . .we are called the Monos of the West. They go from here to Bishop. They traded with one another. . .

I don't know what is going to happen to our children. I wish they would keep the traditions and keep up the Mono tribe. . .

Michael Chiago

Papago
ILLUSTRATOR

Michael Chiago

"When I paint I try to show the pride and beauty of my ancesters" says Papago artist Michael Chiago, who loves to dance as well as to paint. He continued, "The Indian people danced for every occasion; sorrow, joy, war, peace, harvests and many other occasions."

"I have danced most of these dances and have worn many of the Indian costumes." Michael wants all people to appreciate the real beauty of the Indian ceremonies. He uses his painting to portray this beauty and relates: "I hope that my paintings will help people in the future to remember the beauty and dignity of the ceremonies as I know them."

Michael Chiago was born in Kohatk village on the Papago Reservation in Arizona, April 6, 1946. He has learned the Indian dances from his boyhood and began his drawing when very young. He attended the Saint Johns Academy High School at Laveen, Arizona where he won a place in the heart of the teachers and Fathers. The war took Michael into the Marine Corps where he said he "did a hitch" both in Vietnam and at Okinawa, but then returned to his native Arizona where he wanted to pursue his interest and talent in art. Because of his interest in painting, Michael attended the Maricopa Technical School where he had the opportunity to study commercial art and some magazine layout.

It was during a two month dance tour of the East Coast and the New York World's Fair that Michael decided to try capturing the aesthetic beauty of the Indian Dances in his painting.

Chiago says that he is basically self-taught. His primary medium is water color with glaze. This gives his paintings a depth and brilliance similar to egg tempera. I saw one of his paintings on display at the St. Johns Indian Festival, and the art seems surrealistic.

The Women's Editor of the Phoenix Gazette, Mary Metzger says of Michael Chiago, "The vividly-costumed leaping Indian bell dancer comes to life under the skilled brush of Chiago, the Papago artist. One can almost feel the warmth of the crackling fire over which the Indian garbed in bold colors whirls in the air and hear the jangle of the bells clasped around his ankles, so lifelike is Chiago's work."

Michael received a commission from the Heard Museum for a water color of a Papago Indian Village. The Heard Museum is one of the nations finest collectors of Indian artifacts. Mike digs into his memory of childhood for the ideas he portrays of his lively dancers. He was chosen by the St. John's Indian School, a porachial high school, to tour with the famed Indian Dancers throughout Nevada, California and Arizona. They then performed in Niagara Falls, New York City and Massachusetts on the East coast.

For more than a decade Michael has done the Eagle dance and he enjoys recalling the graceful and intricate movements. Very often Michael will visit other pow-wows just to watch the techniques of other Indian dancers.

Mike claims that the techinique he uses is basically one he developed in working with his paints. He uses a special coating when a painting is finished, which gives a unique texture.

Now, Mike works on many of his paintings at night. During the day he is working as a commercial artist at one of the Arizona magazines.He sometimes free-lances. While the smaller paintings take about nine hours to complete, the larger ones often require up to 14 hours to finish. The painting takes patience and persistance.

It was at a special showing of Indian arts and crafts at The Showcase in Casa Grande, Arizona that the officials from the Heard Museum came by and viewed some of Michael's colorful paintings. Frank DeHoney was custom-framing some of Mike's paintings at the time. Chiago says he just happened to be at the right place at the right time, and mother luck took over.

The Heard representatives were so taken with Michael's work they bought three of his dances which were framed as one picture. It was then they commissioned Mike to do the Indian village picture encompassing the animals, the buildings and the Indian people doing the typical chores.

DeHoney, who frames many of Michael's paintings is proud of his friend. He takes special pride in giving the proper background for Chiago's work. It is Mike's friend DeHoney who helped him sell 14 of his recent pictures and has this to say: "I would say that Michael's work is every bit as good as the big names in modern Indian art - David Williams, Robert Draper, Yellow Hair and Yassie." That is a real vote of confidence in this aspiring young artist on the way up.

And Mike is a practical man. He worked for a time as a barber and is licensed in the trade. It was after barbering that he entered commercial art.

Michael is developing a primitive style all his own. He has now gained a real foothold in the art world, he wants to give full time to his art work. And Mary Metzger of the Phoenix newspaper says, "The talent is there -- only Chiago can develop it."

Keep an eye open for this budding Papago artist, who is determined to make a name in the Art and in the Indian world.

Charles Banks Wilson

**Picture of Jim Thorpe in the 1912 Olympics
drawn by Charles Banks Wilson**

Charles Banks Wilson

Few other artists have become so identified with their State as Oklahoma's Charles Banks Wilson. Painter, printmaker, magazine and book illustrator, teacher, lecturer and historian, his work has been shown in over 200 exhibitions in this country and throughout the world. The permanent collections of major museums and galleries contain his paintings and prints of Oklahoma life. These include New York's Metropolitan and Washington's Library of Congress, Corcoran Gallery and the Smithsonian. Oklahoma school children study from a history text containing some 50 of his drawings. The artist's watercolors portraying the southwestern landscape and points of interest have been seen regularly by millions of Americans in Ford Motor Co. publications.

Author and editor of a standard work on the Indian Tribes of Eastern Oklahoma, he is also the illustrator of 22 books and has done pictures for many more. Wilson illustrations enrich such prize winning books as the classic TREASURE ISLAND, COMPANY OF ADVENTURES, Henry's LINCOLN, and the late J. Frank Dobie's personal favorite, THE MUSTANGS.

While writers have said the paintings by Charles Banks Wilson breathe the spirit of the southwest it can be said also, his mural, The Trapper's Bride in the Jackson Lake Lodge, Wyoming, commissioned by the late John D. Rockefeller, Jr. in 1955, ranks among the finest records of the far west's fur trade.

Besides the Oklahoma Press Association's portrait of Will Rogers which was on loan for the Oklahoma World's Fair exhibit, Wilson also did the life portrait of Thomas Gilcrease who established Tulsa's Gilcrease Museum. This museum owns 55 works by the artist. Other portraits include the Washington portrait of the S.G.I.C. of Oklahoma's Scotish Rite Masons, Charles P. Rosenberger. "Osage Orator," is a painting of Charles Whitehorn, one of the last fullblood Osages and long time tribal leader. The Oklahoma painter is best known for his pictures of contemporary Indian life, a project which has engaged him since the early 30's. Undoubtedly his most popular efforts have been in this vein. His "Ten Little Indians" Portfolio has been reproduced in literally every country in the world.

Honored by the U.S. State Department as well as the International Institute of Arts and Letters in Geneva, Wilson makes his home in Miami, Oklahoma. His wife is a member of the Quapaw Tribe, the tribe which was the original owner of what is now the state of Oklahoma.

Charles Banks Wilson's most recent project is the creation of four mural portraits for permanent installation in the State

Capitol, rotunda in Oklahoma City. This is the first state-commissioned art project. The life-size figures include Will Rogers, which was the first to be completed and unveiled October 1, 1964, the Indian Sequoyah, the late U.S. Senator, Robert S. Kerr and the worlds greatest athlete, Jim Thorpe.

Dr. Richard St. Germaine

Lac Courte Oreilles
COMMUNITY - EDUCATOR

Dr. Richard St. Germaine

"I was raised on the Lac Courte Oreilles reservation in northern Wisconsin. I was one of fourteen children, and I was the oldest. There are a lot of demands on one in being the oldest child. I learned at a young age to take responsibility," relates "Rick" St. Germaine.

Dr. Richard D. St. Germaine was born in Idabel, Oklahoma on March 4, 1947. He received his elementary and secondary education in various Indian public and mission schools located in Wisconsin, North Dakota, Wyoming and Utah. He entered Wisconsin State University at Eau Claire in 1965, graduating in 1969 with a Bachelor of Arts Degree in Secondary Education Art Education. He taught and coached athletics at Greenwood High School in Greenwood, Wisconsin from 1969 to 1970, and in 1970-1971, he was director of the Community Action Program (O.E.O.) for the Lac Courte Oreilles Tribe in Wisconsin. He also served as Chairman of the Lac Courte Oreilles Tribal Education Committee, member to the Wisconsin Indian Education Committee and member of the Wisconsin Indian Legislative Committee.

In 1971, Rick received a Ford Foundation Fellowship to pursue his doctoral studies in educational administration and supervision at Arizona State University. In 1972, he received his Master of Arts Degree in Community Education at Arizona State University, and in 1973 to 1975, he was named a special consultant to the Office of Indian Education (U.S.O.E./H.E.W.) as a project evaluation trainer, application and proposal reader, and management consultant. In 1974, he was Co-Chairman of the Sixth Annual National Indian Education Association Convention in Phoenix, and later he was elected to the Board of Directors of the National Indian Education Association and became Treasurer and Executive Committee member to the organization. He is an enrolled member of the Lac Courte Oreilles (Ojibway) Tribe of Wisconsin.

Concerning the current status of his reservation, Rick says:

It is sad to see some of the changes that have taken place on the reservation, but there have been some improvements such as our economic future. There is a lot more self-government. There is a brighter future in terms of tribal self-help. Our tribes are becoming more independent and self-sufficient. Our tribal employees have increased from about 10 to about 250, and we are a small reservation. We are deeply involved in the construction business. We have our own cranberry enterprise. We have a marina, and we have our own school system now. We are constructing a cooperative store and growing in the tourist industry.

One of the beautiful things about this is there is a revival of the spirit of the culture. Our people are moving back to some of the cultural richness of the past, such as tribal marriages, burials, ceremonies, and Indian traditions in our schools.

I want to see the tribe grow economically. I feel we need a more fulfilled life for our tribal members. I think we need to retain the cultural richness of our tribe. It is my hope our tribe will become more self-sufficient.

When asked about influences on his thinking in the past, he replied:

I think my mother mostly influenced me. Her name is Saxon Gouge. She wanted me to get an education and always encouraged me. She was quite a tribal leader herself. She mostly influenced me through her example. She is the kind of woman who is very kind and took in kids into our home, even though we had lots of children. She was one of the few women, the earliest woman, on the tribal council. She was always fair with us.

I think Dr. Thomas Mayhew had a great influence on me. He was one of my teachers in Community Education, one of the finest teachers who ever was. He got involved with his students both in and out of the classroom. He always gave me a lot of encouragement.

WHAT DO PEOPLE THINK OF DR. RICHARD G. ST. GERMAINE?

Says Jim DeHass, an Otoe Indian from Ponca City, Oklahoma:

I know Richard both as a student and as an Indian Administrator. When Rick sees a problem he takes a positive stand and sees it through to its conclusion. He and Randy Eubank put the Indian Education Conference on in Phoenix in 1973, and it has continued since. This is a national conference, bringing national Indian Educators together. Rick has been the president of that group, the National Indian Education Association.

He has inspired many students, and has taken an active part in activities affecting American Indians, not just his own tribe. I think of him as an outstanding leader among the Indian people.

Rick has a rare ability to integrate cultures. He has not lost his own culture, but he has adapted and succeeded in the Anglo culture.

He is one of the finest Indian students I have ever known,'' says Dr. George C. Jacques of the Southwest Regional Center of Community Education. "Rick is very active in a lot of efforts to improve the lot of the Indian people. Because of this some people see him as a radical--which means getting at the roots."

Dr. John E. Walker, Assistant Professor of Supervision and Educational Administration at Arizona State University and Chairman of Rick's doctoral committee says, "He is one of the outstanding leaders in school administration that I know. When Rick came to campus, he was appalled at the lack of empathy that the University had toward Indian students. There were many Indian dropouts at ASU. It was mainly because of a lack of sensitivity to the needs of the Indian students. For example, there were few tutorial programs, and counseling for Indian students was minimal.

"Rick helped organize a tutorial program and guided many of these Indian students. He was also the editor of a newsletter, SKIN, an Indian student newspaper. Rick is a person who believes in people and in worthwhile causes. He did not hesitate to become involved in matters of injustice, and at one time led a march on the ASU campus. He felt the Indian people were getting the short end of the stick. The administration tried to get him to cool it, but he accomplished his aims. He is a real leader. He helped organize the National Conference for Indian Educators, and he got the funds for the gathering."

Rick is married to Arlene Smith, and they have two children-- Ernie and Marcia. The family currently lives at Lac Courte Oreilles, Wisconsin. Rick became president of the National Indian Education Association with headquarters in Minneapolis, Minnesota. He serves also as Director of Education for his tribe. This responsibility includes supervision of higher, vocational education, elementary, secondary, headstart, and health education. As it is obvious from his activities and offices held, Rick is devoted to the improvement of conditions among not only his own people, but also those of all American Indians.

Delbert Broker

Chippawa

BUSINESSMAN

Delbert Broker

I left the reservation as a kid, very very young. I headed to the little town of Royalton, Minnesota. I remember we spent our summers on the Reservation at White Earth, Minnesota. We just bummed around as a kid. We did hiking, watched the singing and dancers, and I like to watch the birds. My old Grandfather used to make bow and arrows out of green willos. We would tie a string on the end of it and had a bow and arrow. My grandfather made baskets out of birchbark. That lasted until I was about 14 years old. Then I moved to St. Cloud, Minnesota, in 1940. I went into the Navy in 1942. I spent about four years in the service.

As all Indians at that time I was exposed to a lot of new ideas and concepts. I thought the exposure amounted to the affluent society. Being as poor as we were at that time, I thought as an Indian person there was something bigger and better that I could do.

AFTER THE NAVY WHAT?

I started school at St. Cloud State. I was on the G.I. Bill. That had a tremendous impact on the Indian people at that time. I wanted to be a coach. I was an active athlete. I was interested in all sports; baseball, ping-pong, football, track. I ran the half-mile and 880. I also did the high-jump. I left school after two years. I had the grand total of 11 credits. I therefore, entered the business world. I spent twenty years in business. That was in St. Cloud.

I started out as a barber. I went to barber school, Moller Barber College, Minneapolis. I barbered for twenty years, total span.

I dabbled in selling stocks and bonds, sold real estate, sold insurance, sold international correspondence courses, and organized a health club. I sold the health club to a friend in St. Cloud.

One of the reasons I went into barbering was that as a young Indian person, by societal standards, I was relegated to the field of menial jobs. My feeling was this, if I was to be successful in either world I had to be successful on my own talents and capabilities.

WHAT ARE THE THINGS YOU LEARNED FROM BARBERING?

The thing I learned most was how to cope with the system. I guess the greatest realization was the fact that in either world, the main issue is economics. I think that holds true today. I think it holds true today that "success" is based on the economic structure.

I have been blessed with the capability of changing my roles in society. I have been able to move into new areas of employment, a new profession without upsetting my basic feelings toward life.

DO YOU HAVE A FAMILY?

My first wife died, when she was young. I have two grown children, a girl and a boy. My son is in construction in Moorhead Minnesota. My daughter works for the telephone company in Fargo, North Dakota.

ANY IDEAS OR SUGGESTIONS FOR INDIAN YOUNG PEOPLE?

I didn't return to college until 1971. I was 46 years old. I was motivated by things I saw that I didn't like, that dealt largely with Indian Education. I did a certain amount of reading while still a barber. I saw this so called Bonanza of Indian Education for Indian people. It was not really Indian Education. I felt it was "white, middle-class academia." This is not to lay the entire blame on the educational system. I would qualify this by saying that the educational institution was the only mechanism we had to gain skills, knowledge, to develop self-worth or identity.

WHAT ARE THE KINDS OF THINGS YOU WOULD LIKE TO SEE IN INDIAN EDUCATION?

My first years in the field of education were spent dealing with the old categorical, historical concept of the Indian. By this I mean the stereotype Indian, paternalistic attitude, that institutions allowed us to operate in.

First, I think Indian people have to find a new point of reference as education relates to Indian people or to Indian societies. My observation was that the primary function of an educational institution is to provide academic knowledge. My second observation is that Indian students enter the academic arena for job gratification. With these two thoughts in mind, I then looked at how can we implement an educational process that will be relevant in a societal setting. From this, I looked at the reservations as a complete and total society, recognizing that reservations are a complete society. This includes the five basic institutions such as religion, education, economics, family, and government. Then I asked myself the question how can we best develop courses or curriculum that would meet those societal needs. I developed a project in Fargo on Indian Education Title IV, which dealt with Indian curriculum at the elementary level. In addition we developed adult basic education programs in high school completion (G.E.D.). We developed a nutritional program. We hid the reading, writing, and arithmetic. We built it into recipes and how to cook food. We also had a sewing class in which we dealt with purchasing, how to buy, and they could see the tangible results. We had a culture class dealing with creative expression. We dealt with the artifacts of the culture, singing, drumming, dancing. The thing that came out of this was that it was a social event that gave peer group reinforcement.

WHAT KIND OF HOPES DO YOU HAVE FOR INDIAN YOUNG PEOPLE?

I feel the Indian people have to recognize themselves as Indians, and not let someone else tell them they are. This is my philosophy. I feel Indianness is an individual thing. It is much like, to draw an analogy, a Christian is a Christian in how he lives Christianity. This is his own individual feeling. I am tired of having Indian people tell them how to be Indian people.

I think it is very simple. I know I am an Indian. I get up before a class, and they want me to tell them they are Indian. They want answers I can't give them. What I mean by feeling "Indian" is that if you have a friend that is really sick, and you tell that friend "I know exactly how you feel," that is a fallacy. No man knows exactly how another feels. How you live "Indian" is what is important.

I am working on a project to bring about relevance to Indian education. Why cannot Indians be studied in Social Work, Sociology, or in content areas? Culture is an intangible thing. By using the societal concept, then we can place tribal government in its proper place. The Indian can study tribal government without worrying about values. We must give him the academic knowledge to go back to the reservation with knowledge about tribal government.

WHAT DO YOU HOPE TO DO?

What the U.S. has done in government policy is take away free enterprise from the Indian people. In doing this they have also taken away professional areas of Indian people. We have no business, industry, salesmen, etc. We need the recognition that we do not have the free enterprise system to develop the professional areas. Where am I to go if I were a professional physicist? Or scientist?

I hope to finish the whole new concept of Indian Education. I hope to get this into the schools.

Dr. Obadiah and Ann Harris

Choctaw/Cherokee
AUTHOR - ADMINISTRATOR

Obadiah Harris

1. My mother was a strong influence in my early childhood. She was a beautiful woman of German descent. She was devoutly religious and taught me to read, using the Bible alone as our reading material. Before ever setting foot inside a school room, I had read the Bible from the first chapter of Genesis to the last chapter of Revelation. Not only that, I had more than a child's understanding, for I shared much of my mother's interpretation of the scripture, which was more literal than esoteric. Also of much influence in my early childhood was my first grade teacher in elementary school. Mrs. Kinney was a sensitive and enlightened teacher of children. From the first day she recognized my special need for reading material beyond the first grade, which she quickly and happily provided. She conferred with my mother very early and gradually expanded my interest and encouraged my love of knowledge.

2. Living in a home of mixed race and bicultural values had both benefits and drawbacks. The benefits are still paying off. The drawbacks are practically forgotten. The ignorant are still among us and prejudice is nourished by the winds of memory. But the greatest enemy I encountered as a child was poverty. After all, money was then and is now the highest value in our society. If you have enough of it everyone respects you, whatever your cultural origin.

3. Tully Morrison, my late father-in-law, would be my choice as a dinner guest. He was probably the best man I ever knew. He came from the worst possible human conditions as a helpless Creek Indian boy and rose to independence and creative self-fulfillment. I never knew a man I admired more fully or loved more deeply.

4. My father influenced me most in my vocational choice. Because of his lack of education, he never let me forget the disadvantages of the uneducated. He led me to believe that education was the royal road to success.

As an Indian boy, he had little opportunity or desire for education. He finished formal school at the eighth grade. His father thought that the work on the farm was more important and that he had wasted enough time.

5. I have always worked with people, the institutions they serve and the communities they live in. Thus I have encountered the common and the uncommon, the universal and the unique problems that impede and improve the race. Whatever difficulty I encounter whether with the individual or the group, the institution or the community, I look within myself to see if there

is anything there that is creating or even attracting the problem. It is suprising how often I can stay at home and find the solution.

6. I hold two B.A. degrees, two Masters and a Ph.D. so the formal should speak for itself. It is the informal that needs explanation. I was the private student of a Jewish sage for seven years. For another seven years I enjoyed the personal tutelage of a great Hindu Philosopher-Mystic. In addition, I studied under my wife's grandfather who was a wise men among the wisest of our early American Indians. Even more important, the informal education is still going on, as the Prophet Isaiah said, "here a little and there a little, line upon line and precept upon precept". Some day our continuing education may reach the infinite dimension, which the Apostle Paul described as going "from glory to glory and from truth to truth". In the meantime, we must struggle with different degrees of ignorance. And for all time we should take the advice of Sri Aurobindo, the great sage of the Modern Orient: "Never by an arrivist".

7. My hopes for the future are to become what I essentially am, an image of the Divine. I wish the same evolutionary fulfillment upon my child and for the children of all and in my own time by the Grace of God in the World and beyond. That alone can establish the foundation for a New World order of peace, harmony, freedom, and love.

8. Compete with yourself mostly. Win the victory against selfishness and greed. Transform the impulses of the uncontrolled unconscious into the rational control of the conscious. Then offer up the conscious to the higher reaches of the superconscious. Let your highest aim be that of personality integration. Everything else will fall into place. Turn more and more to the light and less and less to the darkness. Lead the way to a higher manhood.

Betsy Kellas

Betsy Kellas, Field Representative for the Los Angeles Indian Center's Education Department, reads a story to Maria Barraza, a student in the after-school tutorial program. Betsy, a Hopi from Phoenix, Ariz., now lives in North Hollywood, Calif., and is a graduate of Cal. State University, Northridge.

Hopi

INDIAN CENTER WORKER

Betsy Kellas

WHAT DO YOU REMEMBER OF YOUR CHILDHOOD?

I was born in Winchester, Virginia. I lived there, but did not attend school until we came to Arizona. My grandfather, Albert Poleeson, a Hopi, is a kachina doll maker and lives in Phoenix. I have two sisters and two brothers. One lives in Massachusetts, and the others in California.

I went to school in Phoenix, Arizona until the third grade. We then moved to Tucson, and then on to Lancaster, California in 1962. My father was a tire salesman, and mother worked as a secretary at Edwards Air Force Base. She was a civil service employee.

My childhood was difficult because my folks got a divorce. I didn't like that. Mother remarried soon, and we headed for California. I went to public schools, and really didn't know many Indians. One can easily lose your identity as an Indian. When my mother was a child, my mother lived on the Reservation, Second Mesa. My grandfather was born in Oraibi, Arizona. They sent him to Sherman Institute, Riverside, and Indian School. They changed his name. My grandfather worked in town, but the family stayed on the reservation. He sent money, food and clothing. It was a hard existance.

I attended high school at Lancaster, where I knew only one other Indian. I tried to get into the life of the major culture. At Tucson, they identified me as a Mexican. I asked my mom for a Kachina doll to take a class. She gave it to me, and I really began to tell people I was an Indian.

When I was at College at University of California Northridge, I did a lot of United Native American club work. It was just for Indian students on Campus. I really became involved in it. It was my second year, and I found I wanted to tell people of my Indian heritage. I had a little opportunity to find out who I was. I wanted to talk to other Indians. This was about the Wounded Knee time when many Indians went to the Dakotas. Many students quit school and went there just to help. They asked me to go with them, but that was not my tribe, not my land.

It got me sensitized. I didn't want to be just another number. I got into discussions with other students, about if an incident such as Wounded Knee, would they go home. I wanted to know how they felt. Some did, they found they needed to return to their people. Some are still there.

One time I talked to a counselor, she was an Indian counselor, and she told me I could not go back because I was a woman.

She slammed her fist down on the desk, and it made me angry. I felt I wanted to be identified as an Indian, not just a woman. I felt like quitting school. I was beginning to feel the system too much. I was getting Bureau of Indian Affairs money. I realized getting the money to get educated was just to be part of the system. That is when I was beginning to grow, to find myself. To become educated was the way I felt I could help my people.

I was secretary for the United Native Americans my first year in college. This is when I was around different Indians, Apaches, Sioux, Onieda, Mission Indians from California, and Crees. I did a lot of speaking. I spoke at schools, clubs, and teachers groups. I spoke about all types of Indian topics, and how I felt about being a Hopi. I remember I was speaking to a women's group. They asked "What can we do to help the Indians?". They said they had some used clothing and canned foods. I said as long as they give them just canned foods they don't eat, that is not solving any problems, really not helping. I said what is really needed is education, so that they can help themselves.

I really learned a lot in the Indian Club. I was really motivated. I found myself. I decided I wanted to teach Indian history.

WHAT ARE YOU DOING RIGHT NOW?

I now work for the Indian Centers Inc. Los Angeles, 1127 W. Washington Blvd. I do education field work, as a representative. I help tutor when I have time. I inform Indians of education programs we provide. We have afterschool tutorial from kindergarden through 6th grade. We have gotten so big we can't hold any more. We also have adult education. We give general education development preparation leading to high school diploma. We have a continuation school for dropouts. It is exciting to work in the Center because most of these people have problems. Many of the parents work, and the children only have a mother. They have to work just to keep going. They are examples of the society, of persons shut out by society. They have not been given a chance. They need to be themselves, and they need more than skills. They need to have opportunities to express themselves. The children are so quiet. They cannot come up and tell you what is bothering them. They just hold it inside. They need people who will listen, and find out how they feel. The Indians need to find out how to express how they feel themselves, and let it be known. I never learned about Indian history in the public school history books. Mother never taught us this. The Indian people need a chance to see what the world is about. Then they will know where they are at. They will know they are at the bottom, and how much they have to work to get up where they want to be.

WHAT DO YOU HOPE FOR THE FUTURE?

I hope I have a chance to be around other Indians. I hope for cultural enrichment for myself, and for Indian youth. I want for all the people to work in unity, whether they are Indians, or non-Indians. It is too late to turn back the clock. Since we are going to be here together, lets clean it up. If we don't, there isn't going to be any sanctuary. I just want to teach Indian children. I want to teach them what they are loosing. I want to help them make a comeback. Unless someone tells them, they will never know what they are missing. There is a lot of work needed in Indian history. If Indians don't do it, nobody else is going to do it.

"PEACE!" And Betsy made the Indian sign of peace.

REVIEWING THE STORY

1. Where was Betsy's grandfather born?
2. What does Betsy's grandfather make?
3. Some of the students in Tuscon thought Betsy was of what nationality?
4. What did Betsy take to her classes to show she is an Indian?
5. Where did Betsy become active with other Indian students?
6. How did Betsy feel she could best help the Indian people?
7. Betsy spoke to what kinds of groups about being an Indian, and a Hopi?

UNDERSTANDING THE STORY

1. What schools did Betsy attend?
2. Why did Betsy's grandfather work in town, instead of on the reservation?
3. What was it Betsy wished her mother had taught her?
4. Betsy thinks Indian Children should have a chance to do what?
5. Indian children need people who will ————————————.
6. Betsy wants to teach ————————————.

FINDING SYNONYMS

Choose the correct synonym and write it in the blank following each word.
1. sanctuary
2. employee
3. school
4. secretary
5. slammed
6. system
7. counselor
8. quit
9. heritage
10. quitting

institute	cease
worker	protection
office worker	adviser
hit	tradition
organization	stop

39

Clara Sue Kidwell

Chippawa/Choctaw
LINGUIST - TEACHER

Clara Sue Kidwell

My mother is from White Earth reservation in Northern Minnesota. My father is originally from Southern Oklahoma. My parents went to Haskell Institute in Kansas when it was still Indian Trade and Vocational School. I taught there from 1970 to 1972. I taught American History, Contemporary Affairs, Western Civilization, Logic and Scientific Method.

I am one of three children. My family is in Muskogee, Oklahoma. I was born in William Hastings Memorial Indian Talaquah, Oklahoma. My grandmother lived with the family. She was Choctaw. She grew up in a family which stressed education. My father has traced a Creek ancestor to the Trail of Tears period. My great-grandfather was a judge in the Choctaw circuit court in Oklahoma.

WHAT DO YOU THINK IS IMPORTANT FOR INDIAN PEOPLE TODAY?

It is important for Indian People to be able to live their own lives, in their own communities. They must be able to determine what is in their own best interest. That might involve anything from having weekly pow-wows to training their children in bi-lingual, bi-cultural programs, to managing their own lands and resources. Indian young people have to learn to assume responsibility for carrying on the traditions of their communities. They must make self-determination for Indian communities a reality.

Now, I am teaching at the University of California, at Berkley in the Native American Studies program. I went to the University of Oklahoma. I have my degree in the history of science. My undergraduate degree is in Liberal Arts, literature, philosophy, French, Latin, and History.

ANY POINTERS FOR INDIAN YOUTH?

The seeming rewards of moving into the dominant society, are often offset by the change in life-style (tensions) and changes of values that go along with assimiliation. The sense of identity in belonging to a group, whether family, or an extended family like on the reservation is something that a lot of young people in the majority population are looking for. They emulate the Indian life-style, beads, headbands, communal living, camping out in teepees are examples.

IF YOU COULD HAVE DINNER WITH ANYONE LIVING OR DEAD, WHO WOULD YOU CHOOSE?

My grandfather, my mother's father, whom I never met. That is my Chippawa grandfather. From what I know he was a pillar of the community, organizer. He was into community education generations ago. He kept the yearly baseball tournament together in Ponsford, Minnesota. He was one-quarter French, 3/4 Chippawa. I have this gloried image of a romantic figure in the backwoods. My mother told me he worked in the woods as a lumberman. I'd like to meet the real person that he was.

I don't know that American society will survive in its present state. The simpleness of Indian life-style in regard to American standards generally is something which the majority society may be forced into because of the political and economic unrest in the country. If American society is going to continue to exist, it cannot be at the expense of the environment, and the destruction of identity in a society which alienates people so completely from each other. People are wrecking the environment and hating each other.

ANY MEMORIES OF YOUR CHILDHOOD AS AN INDIAN?

In 1948 they had a big Indian pagaent in Muskogee. My grandmother and I got to ride on a float. It was rather hard not to grow up in a distinctively Indian community. Muskogee is a place where people are proud of Indian heritage. But, we did have a sense of Indian pride. The values I learned from my Grandmother are distinctly Indian values, such as the way my parents live sharing their home, food, generosity with friends, relatives, and sometimes complete strangers. That is a value which is a very integral part of Indian life.

WHAT CAN THE MAJORITY POPULATION LEARN ABOUT THE INDIAN?

Indian people live fairly close to nature. We visited on the reservation in Minnesota during the summers. When I was little, what gripped me was our kerosene lanterns, we slept on feather beds, cooked on wood stove, and drew water from a pump in the kitchen. Life was more simple, much poorer, in terms of material comforts. But life was more free than life in Muskogee. Indians are traditionally respectful of nature, and loved with it. People on the reservation still gather wild rice in Minnesota, fish and hunt deer. Although the standard of life seems much lower, and there are poverty problems, the Indian way of life is at a slower pace. People are more aware of their relationship with nature. A lot of the frustrations and tensions of a competitive life-style in the majority society don't trouble Indian people.''

Veronica L. Murdock

Mohave

President

NATIONAL CONGRESS
OF AMERICAN INDIANS

Veronica L. Murdock

I was born on the Colorado River Indian Reservation in Parker, Arizona. I have five sisters and one brother, and my father is Pete Homer Sr., a Mohave, the tribal chairman for ten years (1954-64). My mother was from Northern California, from the Shasta tribe. They met when my dad attended Haskell, Phoenix Indian School, then University of California Los Angeles. When there he got into the movies. He met mother, Alice Courts, on the movie set. She was a seamstress in the wardrobe department. They fell in love.

I think the most influence came to me when I was in high school. My dad was in tribal politics. Mrs. Agnes Savilla, the first woman on the tribal counsel, had a real impact on my life. She was a good model for me, and encouraged and chaperoned me. She encouraged me to get into Indian youth activities such as the National Indian Youth Council, and student activities.

Of course my parents were encouraging to me. They urged me to get into extra-curricular activities in the high school, such as Future Homemakers of America, and the square-dance group led by an Indian caller, named Morris Sevada, a Navajo. We traveled all over California and Arizona. I was a leader in that group, of which there were about 10 of us. It was mostly Indian girls. Unfortunately, not many boys would participate. I recall, there was one Mexican boy. My mom and dad were always in community activities and encouraged me in leadership.

I began to develop leadership in community development started on the reservation. I was helped by Dr. Spencer and Emily Hatch, from India some years ago. They were instrumental in my leadership development.

I was always involved in sports, such as basketball, rollerskating, softball, baton-twirling, and other sports. One of the funny things I remember in my development, was when we were in school, they didn't have girls sports at the high schools. We were just little squirts. The big girls wouldn't let us. I went to my mom and dad, and said, ''The big girls won't let us play.'' But. I wanted to play, because in Phoenix I had played with my older sisters, and I knew I was good, and wanted to play. I asked my Dad, and he and my mom started a team in Parker, all girls. Most were 13 years and younger. We played in tournaments, Los Angeles tournaments, and at different reservations in Arizona and California. I·played forward, and really enjoyed it.

When we couldn't accomplish things one way I would accomplish it another. In school we didn't have Indian clubs yet. My Home

Economics teacher, Mrs. May Baldridge urged me to organize clubs, and I became president of the Future Homemakers of America. She helped me develop leadership, as did Miss Hubbard, my physical education teacher, and Mr. Bill Brennan, my English teacher.

ANY OBSTACLES YOU RAN INTO?

The only obstacles I ran into was in myself. I lacked self-confidence. You have to build up self-confidence. You get this through your parents, your teachers. The main problem I had was in my math. Algebra was my worst subject. I should have failed. My teacher really helped. I fell behind when I was ill two weeks. I didn't feel any strain or pressure.

I attended college at Arizona State University. I traveled a lot. I got active in the Dawichind Indian Club at ASU. I remained active in sports, basketball and softball. I played pitcher in softball. I went two and one-half years in the college. I worked a lot with the Indian Club, but in my second year I roomed with non-Indians, and that was a whole different situation. That broadened my outlook. We went with different kinds of friends, many non-Indian friends. In college I stayed mostly with Indian friends, but the second year I associated with many types of students. My high school girlfriend, Lois Maha, had graduated from Haskell. She is a Hopi, and got a job in Los Angeles. I spent the summer with her, and decided to work out there. I really got introduced to the work world. That was a funny situation. They wouldn't hire me just for the summer. They didn't have much of a work program. I had to lie about my two years of college. They didn't want anyone who was going to leave. I stayed in Huntington Park, a really fun part of my life. I worked for an insurance company as a secretary. I looked up Dunn and Bradstreet, made out reports and forms.

From there I came back to Arizona State University. I was in business administration and physical education. I got married. I married Leonard A. Enos, who was killed in Vietnam in 1963. That was a long time ago.

Then I started working for the Bureau of Indian Affairs. I found I just couldn't get back to my studies. I was a dictaphone transcriber, in the Personnel Department, in the Phoenix office.

The one thing I learned there is that when you have a job there, you do just that job. If you try to help other people they discourage, unless you change your field. That was not a challenging job, but I learned the job well. It wasn't what I wanted to know.

My tribal chairman contacted me and asked me if I would like to return to the Reservation, and interview for a job. Mr. Dempsey

Scott was the chairman. The job was a neighborhood youth corps director, under the Great Society program of Presidents Kennedy and Johnson. It was working with school youth, and a jobs program for low income people. One of the main concerns was my youth. Some wondered if I could handle the adult segment of the program. I think I handled it well. I went out, and found out about the program. We had a very successful program. We made the transition to new additions of programs, both tribal and federal programs.

There is a significant part of my life. During a summer I met a young man whom I had known in the L.A. area. His name is Myron Murdock, a Kickapoo. Myron is presently working with our Adult Education program on Colorado River Reservation. He is really smart. He is a counselor-teacher. He works with youth and adults. An interesting thing is he lived in L.A. for 12 years, and the Reservation was a real shock for him. He expected to find a fence or something around the Reservation. He calls it his home now. He had one daughter eight years old, named after my mother, Alice Renee Murdock. She is a sweet child.

After I had served for three years in Neighborhood Youth Corps, I got involved in Tribal politics. I turned 25 on December 25, 1968, two days before the election. I had filed as a candidate for Tribal Counsel--there are 9 on the Council.

I never expected to be elected, let alone become Vice-Chairman. Then the Vice-Chairman was selected by the Council, elected. Here comes a 25 year old, who had little experience, but the people asked me if I would accept the Vice-Chairman post, and I knew I had the capability and knowledge to do the job. I did not know the scope and responsibility but I learned it. I served as Vice-Chairman from 1969 to 1972.

That same year 1969, I got involved in the National Congress of American Indians. I was elected Phoenix Area Vice-President. There I served for 1 year. Next year I was elected National recording secretary. This was voted on by all the tribes. I was re-elected for two years in a row. I remained active, but not in an office. In 1975 I was elected First Vice-President, and then in 1977 I was elected President. Three men ran against me. I think there were 8,000 votes and I got about 5,600. 141 tribes are represented. The National Congress of American Indians is the oldest and largest Indian organization in the United States. It has about 150 tribes members now, and about 4,000 individual members.

I am most involved in Legislation. This deals with water rights, land rights, treaty rights, and related problems. We are working on organizationally to increase the activities of all tribal leaders throughout the country. We help them get involved in the education of the non-Indians, and in public relations related to the Indian people's problems.

One thing I would like to see is a plan developed by tribal people, and our other leaders that can address this legislation. We need a projection into the future. This is the tip of the iceberg, there are so many problems. If we don't we will be in greater problems. Indian people have looked to tribal leadership and national leadership to address these vital concerns.

I think this Presidency was my most significant contribution. I consider my outspokenness is most appreciated. I say what I feel. I hope other people respect this. At least I let other people know what I feel and think. I hope the other tribes appreciate this. If others disagree, I sit down with them, and we exchange ideas on a one to one. I am not afraid to ask for advice, and I am not afraid to take advice. I do not have all the answers, but I hope my leadership will help our Indian people.

I have served on my Council, the Colorado River Council for ten years, to end in 1980. I serve on a council member basis, not a full time job. I believe they appreciate my national leadership, and have given me their moral and financial support. My family, husband, sisters, daughter are understanding and make my job a lot easier.

Ten years from now I would like to be still working with young people. Not on a full-time schedule, but dealing with young people developing their talents and abilities.

Terrance F. Leonard

Pima
CARTOGRAPHER - ENGINEER

Terrance F. Leonard

WOULD YOU TELL ME ABOUT YOUR CHILDHOOD, TERRY.

I was born on the Salt River Pima-Maricopa Reservation in Arizona. I was raised by my grandparents. My grandfather was a police commissioner for the Reservation and we lived at the Agency until he retired, about 1958. Both of my grandparents were from the Pima tribe. They had a great deal of influence in my growing up. My grandmother helped to recognize a problem and to deal with it positively. She helped me work out problems of right and wrong and to share the experience with others. Her name was Monica. She was a very religious person. Her greatest influence in that area is that I learned to show respect --especially qualities of life. She made me realize how important it is to help others in need of help.

As a child I attended the Salt River Bureau of Indian Affairs day school. The nickname I got as a boy, because of my mischief, was "terrible Terry." When I was in the first grade we had a contest. The one who got the multiplication table best got a fire-truck, and I got to a thousand first. I picked up many kinds of awards while going to school, even though I was the youngest in my class. The saddest part of school was that my grandfather died of a heart attack when I was in 7th grade. I became the head of the family. I had two brothers and a sister plus our first cousins to be responsible for, plus my grandmother.

I had to work hard. I did field work, irrigation and did dairy work on a farm. My uncle was handicapped, since he had his leg amputed, so he couldn't work. I worked at odd jobs after school, just to make a living. Basically my elementary years were happy.

I got involved in art, sketching, cartooning and work in pen and ink. I was in the Boy Scouts. I think I was the first to become an Eagle Scout from our community. I was the captain of the safety patrol, wearing our white helmets. I got some awards for my drawing.

TELL ME ABOUT YOUR HIGH SCHOOL.

I went to Junior High and the High School in Mesa, Arizona. I recall the 8th grade because it was so different from the Bureau School. The subjects and the requirements were so different. They asked what kind of courses I wanted and what I wanted to be.

Then I joined the Future Farmers of America and took agriculture too. I took mechanical drafting, but didn't do too well. I took it not knowing I would be a professional draftsman.

The biggest impact was my agricultural class. I remember one teacher that influenced me was Mrs. LaBarron, my English teacher. My high school counselor Merrill Smith, who is still there, was a great help, and stuck with me through many problems. He kept me in a positive attitude, which was so important in the senior class. We were really good friends. We still are. Mrs. LaBarron said I could express myself in words and I was able to set some long range goals. She called me idealistic. I was involved in sports: wrestling and football. When I was in high school I was on the honor roll.

We did surveying, drawing and sketching of farms and I got involved in entomology--the study of insects. In my high school senior year, I competed nationally and regionally in the F.F.A. contest. I was the secretary and then the vice-president of the Club for our Mesa chapter. I judged livestock, meats which were my two specialties. I was voted the outstanding senior for our Chapter in 1964. I had an A average, which helped me get into college. My goal at that time was to become an agriculture teacher.

I went to the University of Arizona to become a teacher of agricultural education. I got three scholarships in order to go. I was there two years. Then I came home. At that time I got married and I had family responsibilities. I married Donna Miguel, who was my high school sweetheart. She had the same kind of interests I had and was the oldest in her family. Her special field is teaching, elementary education. We now have four children, Michael, Dennis and Terisa and Trina. Our little one has a rare kidney disease and unfortunately it is terminal.

Then in 1965 I started working as a surveying aide. I was what is called a rearchainman. I became more interested in what we were surveying. I read blueprints, maps and made the field calculations. In order to better understand my work, I took courses in surveying at Phoenix College. I spent about two years in the field. Then one day they asked me to do some printing, drafting. It was just to test me. That started my drafting career. I became proficient at civil-engineering drawing. But, I wasn't yet happy with that. I wanted to design something. I have since designed many highways, sub-divisions airports and bridges. From 1965 to 70 I spent with four private engineering firms and the state highway department. I was in planning and design.

It was interesting. At the highway department I got into aerial photography--surveying from the air. That is where I picked up the title of cartographer. It was then I got involved in computers. To analyze the latitude and longitude we used the computer for analysis. We converted a lot of township corners, to state plane-coordinates, for mapping purposes. After I left the Highway department I went to work for Trico International, the engineering component of MacCulloch Industries. I did land planning, for Lake Havisu-City, Fountain-Hills and Pueblo West, Colorado. I did a lot of traveling and am still doing that. My job was to take ground to plan it into a city, making a master plan.

During this time I was doing similar work for our Salt River Reservation. In order to improve my work, I took specialized courses at Phoenix College, Mesa Community College and Arizona State University. These include classes in real estate law, real estate land development & urban planning and design. My new interest was law, particularly real estate law.

This led me to a position with the Economic Development Administration for the Salt River Reservation and Ft. McDowell Reservation. I worked closely with the tribal governments. Even in high school I was involved with our Tribal Council, community government. I was on the education committee and served as president for two years.

This experience was significant because I visited the boarding schools of the Bureau of Indian Affairs. This was to assist our students from our community. That led to my getting involved in establishing an INTER-TRIBAL SCHOOL BOARD. The official title is the Phoenix Inter-Tribal School Board. There are four off the reservation boarding schools, with a total of 55 schools involved. I helped initiate this Board, and am the current Chairman of it. The board covers five states: Arizona, California, Nevada, Utah and one school at Lawrence, Kansas, Huskell Junior College. The purpose is to assist the Bureau of Indian affairs in policy formation for the schools. We are involved in budgets, rules and regulations and plant maintenance. I have come to realize that the boarding school student can be the loneliest person on earth. Even to make it through the year takes a lot of guts. I am very committed to these youth and in turn, I hope that something we may have said will help that student realize his or her dreams.

All these activities I did on a volunteer basis. I did it because I wanted to make a contribution, I wanted to be involved. This got me active in national organizations such as National Congress of American Indians, National Indian Education Association, many Indian schools throughout the country. I did most of this in the last ten years.

We were instrumental in establishing the Division of Indian Education in the Arizona State Department of Education. I had no idea I would end up as head of that division which I am today. I felt since I was spending so much time with education, I decided to get directly involved. I felt I could help relations between the youth, the tribes and the state. Everything I do has as my objective helping young people.

I was driving down the road, and remembered this was the last day to apply for the position of DIRECTOR OF INDIAN EDUCATION. I applied because I felt I should be involved in the education of our Indian youth. I got the job, appointed by Dr. Weldon P. Shostall. I competed with some top talent and was the youngest Director of a Division in the Department. I was only 27 years old at the time.

WHAT HOPES AND DREAMS DO YOU HAVE FOR INDIAN YOUTH?

The basic hope I have is I want to see youth recognize their own problems, approach themselves with respect, whatever the results will be, they must work to help their own people. They must improve their status in life. All these tools, all the education should be used to help the Indian youth develop to that point. I have the same dream and hopes for my own children.

My personal goal is to finish the University and obtain a law degree. I have found the need to be trained in law, relative to the many kinds of work I have done over the years. It is especially important when I go before the House or Senate appropriations committee. Then I request and present our needs. Training in law is always useful to present the problem.

Says Bernard Casey, a professor in history at Mesa Community College, Mesa Arizona, "He recognizes a problem in the gap between tribal life and industrial society. Terry is capable of working with the business world and is quite successful in the field of cartography, especially aerial map making. Terry is on the Salt River Pima-Maricopa community council. His goal is to keep pride in the Indian heritage, while still helping the Indians cope with modern society. For example, Terry told me of an occasion when his telephone was out of service for almost a month. The problem had been that one of the tribal members decided he didn't like the telephone pole on his property and just went out and chopped down the telephone pole. The whole corner of the reservation was out of service for some time. The first time Terry had ever been tenting, was when he as an adult used a tent of mine, to go on an outing to Northern Arizona. Terry is one of the bright young leaders of the Salt River Reservation."

"Terry has a degree in architecture and I would say is one of the young upcoming Indian leaders, I think we will hear more from him in the future. As Director of Indian Education for the state of Arizona he is knowledgeable about federal programs and statutes that directly aid Indian children for the state.'' says Gay Lawrence, Education Program Specialist in the Arizona State Department of Education.

Joanne Linder

Cherokee
ADULT BASIC EDUCATOR

Joanne Linder

Joanne Linder was born in Muskogee, Oklahoma. The family lived between Fort Gibson and Talaquah. "There were seven children in the family. I was the youngest. My father was a druggist. Dad met my mother up in Missouri when he was going to school. My mother was French & Irish and disinherited by the family for marrying an Indian. Mother taught in a little one room school. She had not finished the 'eighth grade. It was a little community, Linder's Bend. There is still a family cemetery there where the parents and grandparents are buried."

TELL ME A LITTLE ABOUT YOUR CHILDHOOD.

My grandparents provided horseshoeing for the community. They had a number of Blacks who worked for them. My grandparents came over the Trail of Tears from North Carolina. They did not like to talk about it or any of their past. Chatauqua players related the story of early Cherokee life in Georgia. Her father was a health officer. The Cherokees there were very careful of the white settlers whom they let into the community. The chiefs and councils saw two problems arising. One was with the blacks. They made it capital punishment if they intermarried. The other was they advised marriage with white people as soon as they could. Our family declared only 1/32 Cherokee when they were enrolled at Talaquah. They seem reluctant to admit to "being Indian", since they were handsomely fair with black hair and gray eyes.

Because there are few full-blood Cherokees outside of the group at Talaquah, inter-marriage meant there are many part-Cherokee.

My childhood wasn't very colorful or happy. My father died when he was 42. My two brothers were put in an orphanage at Sequoia, Oklahoma. Each time we visited it appeared more sad. My mother wanted to keep me with her and she thought housework was the best way to do it.

My brother John R. did go through college at Stillwater, Agricultural and Mechanical. My other brother died at seventeen of appendicitis. We had poor medical care and, of course, no penicillin, then.

My life was patterned after my older sister who was a secretary at the Indian Hospital at Claremore. That was the home of Will Rogers. He was also a Cherokee.

I worked my way through the Junior College at Wilberton, Oklahoma. I finished at Oklahoma A. & M. at Stillwater. I started in secretarial training, but fortunately a counselor advised me into adding teacher training. I had been a business teacher eight years in Colorado when I became interested in adult education with Manpower in Phoenix. We were the very first staff of the program. That was when I became interested in working full-time with Indian groups. There is so much hidden skill and talent behind shyness with Indians. In most cases all that is needed is a little spark or encouragement. I enjoy trying to give that spark and help needed. The reward is most gratifying.

DO YOU REMEMBER ANY SUCCESS STORY?

I worked for two years at Ft. Defiance, Arizona, with the Navajo as the business education instructor. Many of the students did get civil service rating. I helped Indians get jobs on the reservation when they did not want to leave.

The most impressive and rewarding experiences was seeing a 53 year old Navajo woman who was deserted by an alcoholic husband, leaving three children in the home, she learned secretarial skills well with no previous training. She learned typing, filing and bookkeeping from the beginning. She was then employed by the Navajo Police Department at Window Rock. She became a fingerprint expert, along with her regular office job. That took a lot of courage, I thought, as she had to attend with younger women in her classes.

Most of the students I worked with were on welfare, in our Phoenix Manpower program. The proudest moment of their lives was when they became employed and independent.

WHAT KIND OF HOPES DO YOU HAVE FOR INDIAN WOMEN?

In most cultures the Indian women were the head of the family. They did make major decisions. We don't often think about that. This is especially true of the Navajo women. I think they realize they must now train and become interested in education along other lines. They must be more concerned about completion of education for their children in order for them to successfully live in the present day.

My philosophy is also that of Elizabeth White, a noted Hopi educator; that little is accomplished crying over the past. Instead, I feel we must take the good points from the white culture and the Indian culture, blend them together for a successful and happy future. I like the title of and philosophy of Elizabeth White's book **NO TURNING BACK**. And there is none for any culture.

WHAT ARE SOME OF THE THINGS YOU ARE DOING NOW?

As Director-Coordinator of the Hualapai and Havasupai Adult Education Program I hope to restore the neglected and almost extinct native skills of pottery and basketmaking of the two tribes. They even wove rabbit-skin coverlets and rugs. They did books and Indian moccasins, almost nonexistant now except as keepsakes in the family.

They seem to feel they should keep this knowledge as secret from Anglos. I think this is tragic as they also keep them secret from future generations. We are trying to restore these arts and crafts skills through adult education. This is in addition to trying to make these skills financial, profitable for supplimental funds. The income is sparce already. Classwork encourages cooperation and working together in classes. Indians then learn understanding between families. This experience can eliminate jealousy and prejudice. Many Indian leaders say Indians are sometimes their own worst enemies. Learning cooperation in our classes does contribute to their individual success establishing Indian identity.

The present community college concept is to direct courses toward family living as well as occupational skills. An example of this is cooking classes, including diabetic diets and health food planning. The basic four foods are emphasized. Silversmithing leathercraft, ceramics and mixed media crafts interest most everyone in the community. The young Indian women are becoming interested in the older and forgotten crafts. These two tribes show great interest in improving their skills and economy through educational programs.

New interests will improve the mental health and a happier outlook of the Indian community. It will give encouragement to participate in off reservation work and living. Skills and knowledge always improves the self-confidence needed by the Native Americans.

Joanne Linder was seated at a table taking orders for the Indian Suzy BelleDolls made by the Hualapai (wall-a-pie) Indian Tribe. The occasion was the 18th Indian Education Conference held at Arizona State University. She was thousands of miles from her home in Muskogee, but is contributing her knowledge and skills to the improvement of the lot of Native Americans. She is using adult education to improve the economy of the Grand Canyon tribes.

Peter MacDonald Sr.

Navajo

Chairman
NAVAJO TRIBAL COUNCIL

Peter MacDonald Sr.

"That young man, Peter, has ability and will go someplace with his life" I said to a faculty member at Bacone College, Muskogee Oklahoma, at that time the only Indian College in the United States. I was serving as Dean of the Faculty and had this bright young Navajo in a Speech class, a freshman group. That was 1949.

That young man with a winning smile and shining teeth who spoke with a firm, stentorian, booming voice was **Peter MacDonald, Sr.**, now the Chairman of the Navajo Nation, made up of 140,000 American Indians in parts of New Mexico, Utah and Arizona. Peter leads a tribe where the annual personal income averages $900 and where the birth rate is highest of any minority group in the United States.

Peter's story is a dramatic one. Born at Teec Nos Pos, meaning Cottonwoods in a Circle, Arizona on December 16, 1928, his father was Daghalani Begay, (Many Whisker's Son), and his mother was Glahhabah, (Many Warriors Over the Hill). Peter's maternal granduncle Deshna Clah Chischilli was the second Tribal Chairman of the Navajo Tribal Council. So Peter comes from a family with leadership abilities. He is married and has five children.

I remember that Peter came to the Bacone High School in Muskogee and completed his work in 1949. That was the year we had Warner Brothers on campus when they made the movie **Jim Thorpe-All American** and Peter was one of the "extras." Peter saw education as the ladder for his success and completed an Associate of Arts in Social Science at Bacone College, an American Baptist Mission College. Approximately 1/3 of the leadership of the Indian tribes had come from his little Indian College, according to the claims of the college administration.

Peter determined he would become an engineer. He entered University of Oklahoma at Norman and by 1957 had obtained the Bachelor of Science degree in Electrical Engineering. He had worked his way through much of his college education. Still wanting to improve himself and prepare for future leadership. Peter entered graduate studies at the University of California at Los Angeles and studied intermittently from 1958 through 1962.

MILITARY SERVICE

Peter entered the United States Marine Corps during World War II in 1944 and was honorably discharged as a corporal in

1946. He relates that he was a member of the famous "Navajo Code Talkers" in the South Pacific.

Peter was a member of the Bacone Indian singers and traveled with the group through many of the northern states, singing mostly in churches. The group was led in Indian sign language by Richard West, the Director of Art at Bacone and the inspiring pianist the late Mary West. The group used the colorful Navajo costumes, wearing the shining silver belts to complete the outfits. The Indian Dances were part of the program and Peter would sing Navajo songs in the high pitched tone.

PETER WORKS UP THROUGH THE RANKS

Peter can claim to have had a variety of rich work experiences. Following his training in electrical engineering at University of Oklahoma, Peter served as Project Engineer and a member of the Technical Staff for the Hughes Aircraft Company in El Segundo, California. Then from 1963 until 1965 he was the Director for Management Methods and Procedures for the Navajo Tribe at Window Rock, Arizona. He had returned to his people and intended to make a dent on the tribal leadership by using his talents. His break came when he became in 1965 the Director of the Office of Navajo Economic Opportunity for the Navajo Tribe at Fort Defiance, Arizona. He administered millions of dollars in funds and became known as a responsible administrator. This was under the administration of President Lyndon Johnson and his "War on Poverty." Peter was making a name for himself and the elders trusted him and his judgment. He was at home in the white-man's world and in the home of the Navajo Indians, his people.

Peter felt he was ripe for major leadership in the Navajo Nation. He campaigned for the Navajo Tribal Chairmanship in 1970 and won the election. He campaigned hard and had stiff competition. But he had won the confidence of the people. He had worked up through the ranks. Peter served as Chairman of the Navajo Tribal Council until 1975 when he was re-elected to that post. He still serves in that important capacity.

CIVIC LEADER IN THE UNITED STATES

Peter MacDonald became the first Indian to be appointed by the Governor of New Mexico to the Advisory Board of the Department of Development for the State of New Mexico. But, Peter is very much a part of the Window Rock community. He is an active member of the Window Rock Baptist Church and President of the Brotherhood. He serves as Executive Chairman of the Navajoland Boy Scouts of America and is a member of the Quarterback Club, the high school booster club. He enjoys working with young people.

In 1974 **Time Magazine** cited Peter as "One of the 200 Rising American Leaders." He was inducted into the Engineering Hall of Fame at the University of Oklahoma in 1975. He is listed in Who's Who in America and Who's Who in the West. But one of the things Peter enjoys most is leading the Navajo Nation band at the Pasadena Rose Parade on his beautiful white horse, Roany. He wore the velvet maroon shirt with multi-colored bandana, with all of the band and its leaders wearing the bright silver belts. The band numbered over 100 and Peter proudly led the group. In the 1975 Rose Parade Peter and I renewed acquaintance after 25 years.

When Peter was 14 years old he got a job at the railroad office. Someone had told Peter "Just go to the Army office and you can get a card that says you're 18. Then take the card to the Railroad office and they'll hire you." Peter followed instructions and the man said, "Show up tomorrow." Now Peter had a job he wanted, he had a card and he was a railroad worker.

Peter worked hard. He got homesick and tired. But he did not quit. In fact, he worked four months nailing down railroad tracks. He found he could do the work other men could do because his grandfather had taught him how to work hard.

PETER'S GRANDFATHER

Peter's father died when he was two. So Peter lived with his grandparents. His grandfather was named Daghalani Begay and was a Medicine Man. The Grandfather knew the Beautyway Ceremony--called "Hozhoji" in Navajo. Grandfather Begay wore his hair tied back in a knot behind his head, like many of the elders do. Peter remembers that his grandfather made him get up in the morning each day and run for a distance outside the hogan. Sometimes when there was snow, the grandfather would make Peter take off his shirt and roll in the cold snowflakes.

Peter learned to tend the sheep, for that was the livelihood for the tribe. Sometimes his fingers felt like they were frozen. Peter's grandfather made him work hard, for he did not want Peter to be weak or lazy. His grandfather would make him hitch up the wagon and get barrels of water for the sheep. Often, Peter and his grandfather would take a walk. They would talk together and this is how Peter learned the wisdom and philosophy of this old Medicine Man. Many times, Peter thought about dropping out of school. But he did not.

PETER GROWS UP

Peter recalls that when he was about 13 he took off for Dolores, Colorado where he got a job in a sawmill. He began to think about becoming an engineer. Peter enjoyed earning the money and after a few months he decided to return home. He and his grandfather traveled around on horseback. Like many of the Navajo, Peter learned to hitch up the horse to the wagon, which they often took to the trading post. He learned some of the legends and the songs while he and his grandfather rode along in the wagon. Then, Peter heard that they were hiring workers for building a big pipeline which was to run across the reservation. He went to the job and signed up. This was another push on his road to becoming an engineer. Then, he heard they were hiring workers on the line up north in Oregon. He had never been so far from home, but here was a chance to travel. With his determination he headed for Oregon and got a job with the Union Pacific Railroad.

THE CODE TALKERS

At the age of 15, Peter became a Marine. He looked older than his age. The United States at that time was at war with Germany, Italy and Japan. The Marines were trying to figure out a way to talk in a secret code to each other over radios, without being understood by enemy forces. Then the idea was presented - - "Why not use the Navajo language?" That was the key. Many of the Navajos said they would help. They made a secret code in Navajo and talked over radios so that the Germans, Italians and Japanese could not understand a word. Peter became one of these "Code Talkers." He had to memorize a long list of more than 400 English words and the Navajo word that would be used for every one. "Bomber" was "buzzard" in Navajo. "Patrol plane" was the word for "crow", and "dive bomber" was "gini" the word for chicken hawk. Peter found the work interesting and exciting. It also helped him with his spoken and written English. This was to come in handy in the years ahead when he would be meeting Congressmen and Senators representing the Navajo Nation.

SHEEP HERDING THEN OFF TO SCHOOL

Peter returned home safely from the war. His mother fixed him big steaming pots of mutton stew and the Indian fried bread which Peter loved to eat.

Peter's family now had a small herd of sheep. His family once had many sheep, but the government people had come and told them they could not have so many sheep, that they were eating too much grass. That made things really difficult for the Navajo. Peter's grandfather had told him, "My grandson, you now have to be sure that you get an education. Your family is poor and it is very hard to make a living with sheep and livestock."

Peter heard from some friends that there is a Baptist Mission school that is for training Indians at Bacone College, Muskogee, Oklahoma. When Peter's mother learned of Peter's desire to go to school, she one day left the hogan and went to the local trading post. There she sold her best turquoise necklace and jewelry and helped pay for Peter's bus ride to the school in Oklahoma.

From then on, Peter had one success after another. And we know the rest of the story, how he became the Chairman of the Navajo nation. He became Chairman in January 1971 -- just following his 42nd birthday.

Peter's theme for the tribe has been "We must do things for ourselves." He has to spend much time in Washington, working on behalf of the Navajo people. He works for better health, better housing and better jobs.

What do people who work with Peter think of him? Here is what his attorney says of Peter --

"Peter is the only Indian leader of my acquaintance that transcends Indian problems in the Indian world. **That** characterizes the man. I think he is the kind of person people make a mistake about sometimes, because they try to corner him, and put his back to the wall. He is one of the few Indians dealing with Washington Senators who will not be put off by a pat on the back, or lunch in the Senate dining room." says Mr. George Vlassis, the office of the General Counsel for the Navajo nation since 1971.

Peter is trying to live up to his grandfather's hopes for him. He believes the Navajo nation should be as self-sufficient as possible. He feels Navajos should find ways to have a full life without having to get help from welfare, the Bureau of Indian Affairs and that they should have their own Public Health Service. He wants to work with all people, but his reminder is "WE MUST DO THINGS FOR OURSELVES." . . . Peter got the tribe to build a factory where the Navajo workers make glasses right on the reservation.

The company, called Navajo Optics is just a beginning. Peter is working to bring the good life to the Navajo Nation.

Someday a really great biography will be written of this Indian leader.

I often say the test of a man's character is how he treats his secretary. This is what Ada P. Bluehouse has to say about Peter MacDonald:

"I've worked for many executives and they all have different styles and approaches in dealing with their jobs and responsibilities.

I found Chairman MacDonald a unique personality, easy to get along with but a much more complex individual than at first glance. He is first of all a warm person, very informed and treats all his guests, whether be high ranking officials or just the average person with the same courtesy, respect and tolerance. He treats his staff with openness, and a great deal of reliance for their views and opinions.

As to decisions, he does not make hasty decisions and always have one or two options ready if the first one doesn't go too well.

In human terms, he is not heavy handed and I have not seen him hold grudges against anyone. As to his power as Chairman, he doesn't throw his weight around, so to speak. Instead he uses his own knowledge as a person and uses a great deal of diplomancy in dealing with people.

He has obvious distaste for political trade offs, he just likes to do things because he believes they are right."

Dr. John Tippeconnic, III

Comanche/Cherokee
EDUCATOR - PROFESSOR

Dr. John W. Tippeconnic, III

I was born in Oklahoma, in 1943. Soon after that we moved to a place near Gallup, New Mexico . . My parents were educators in the Bureau of Indian Affairs. My dad was principal of the Mexican Springs School and my mother was the head cook at the school. I started out in the public school the first two years.

I have a large family. I have five brothers and two sisters. I am the youngest boy in the family. We were a close family. We did things together, like sports. My dad was very interested in sports. We had our own team, like the Kennedys, and were very close in that way.

While at this school, some of my older brothers went off to a Methodist Indian boarding school at Farmington, New Mexico. One by one they went to that school. We would visit them periodically and see them perform.

When I was in the second grade, my parents were transferred to a B.I.A. school named Canoncito Day School. Again dad was principal. I went to school there through the seventh grade. This was a happy experience. I think this experience sparked my interest in education especially in administration. I was the only upper grade student, the only seventh grader. This meant my dad taught me and other classes.

I was helping dad teach other students, even helped in the kitchen and some of the administrative things. With the closeness of the family, it helped me develop responsibility. It helped me view and accept work habits and learned to get things done.

The person who had the most influence on me was my dad. It was a growing experience to see him perform. This was a day school with my dad involved in the community. It was exciting to see my parents lead. The community would come to my folks for help, advice and my parents would assist them. This was an important experience and helped me develop a humanistic viewpoint on life. My dad stressed education and I think he stressed this because he was a product of the governments educational policy. He too went to the bureau boarding school and the approach then was assimilation into the mainstream as soon as possible. The school relfected this. Anything Indian was downgraded, was not to be done in the school setting.

They could not speak their language, could not practice their customs, their hair was cut and many times they were given non-Indian names. They aimed at "De-Indianizing" the students.

At that time the Indian child had to make a decision. They had to reject their Indian culture, their Indian way of life or they could go back to it if that was possible. My dad was a product of this environment. He had a lot of unpleasant memories of that process. He recognized the value of an education and he tried to get that across to me.

There was no direct effort of my parents to teach me some of the aspects of the Indian culture, the Indian way of life. My dad is Commanche and my mother is Cherokee. They did not prevent me from learning about the culture, the way of life of the Indian people. I learned this by living in the community and by observing and growing up with other Indians, mostly from the Navajo tribe. Dad did not want us to go through the unhappy experiences he had.

Although we did not have a "Christian home," the values could be interpreted to be Christian in nature. Things like accepting responsibility, like alcohol was not accepted. My dad smoked cigars, but smoking was not practiced in our home. In the educational process of the family, I think my family are to be commended, for they sacrificed to get the children through school. There was a time when three of my older brothers were in college at the same time and they had no outside financial assistance. At home they really sacrificed to get us through school.

WHAT HANDICAPS HAVE YOU ENCOUNTERED?

At Oklahoma, just being an Indian, at times I felt discriminated against. Sometimes it was quite open. One example, in a small town in Oklahoma a couple of friends and I were refused service in a restaurant. Being away from the family was hard. Our family had close relationships and it was bad going away to boarding schools. Once I graduated from college and was working as a professional, people did not look at me just for what I could do. Perhaps they looked at me as what I represented as "an Indian." In order to be accepted I had to perform at or beyond the level of others. I had to prove myself.

IF YOU COULD HAVE DINNER WITH ANYONE LIVING OR DEAD, WHO WOULD YOU CHOOSE?

I think I would like to sit down with my dad and have a real good discussion of the education of the Indian today. He comes from a background of wide range in terms of development. He lived in a tepee. He knows the people, Commanches, the culture, the history and what their socialization process was in the tribe.

He was involved in schools as a student, teacher and administrator. Because of this he was involved in both worlds, the Indian world and the non-Indian world. I'd like to discuss ways we could make education more relevant for Indian students. I would also like to discuss how we can develop a better understanding of the Indian by the non-Indian. To accept the Indian for what he is and appreciate his heritage and way of life. We need to know where we are coming from and have a philosophical base. Program activity comes next.

One thing I have been frustrated about is at times in the Indian community there is a lack of professionalism. There sometimes is a lack of carrying out responsibility and this frustrates me. I can understand it because of the culture and the way of life. In some cases individuals think that just being an Indian is enough. But, there is a conflict . . the non-Indian world expects people to perform in a certain time-frame. You must do this today-that tomorrow, and in a certain way and according to their standard. In the Indian world emphasis may not be placed on these things. Time is not an emphasis, but is more casual in the Indian world. You go about your own pace. If you can do it tomorrow that is o.k.

WHAT ARE SOME OF YOUR HOPES FOR THE FUTURE?

My hope is that we can develop a strong educational influence in the Indian Community. I want to see educational programs that will take into account the individual student and where he comes from. I want to help develop community based programs that will involve parents and other community members. My hope for my boy is to create a learning environment where he can grow with an open mind and have an understanding of the other person. I hope he can make decisions for himself based upon his own interests and the interests of others. I want him to recognize he is an Indian, be proud of it and I want him to develop an understanding of the Indian community. I want him to decide what he wants to be, not me.

John Tippeconnic is a graduate of Oklahoma State University, Stillwater, where he majored in Secondary Education. He went on to school at University of New Mexico, Albuquerque, where he worked in guidance and counselling. At Flagstaff, Arizona, he studied Community Education at Northern Arizona University. He got his Master of Education and Ph.D. in Educational Administration at Pennsylvania State University in 1975 where he did a study of Teacher-Pupil control ideology in Navajo schools.

John became first Assistant to the President and the Vice-President of the new Navajo Community College at Tsaile, Arizona. He worked up through the ranks from a Social Studies, Junior High and Elementary teacher at the Tuba City Boarding School.

Dr. Tippeconnic is now the Director of the Center for Indian Education at Arizona State University, Tempe, Arizona where he teaches courses in Indian Culture, in the Special Education Department. He is married to Rosita Blatchford and lives with his wife and son, John William Tippeconnic IV. John III, is a member of Phi Delta Kappa, American Indian Education Association and the American State University Center for Indian Education which trains persons in the American Indian cultures.

Vivian Ayoungman

Canadian Blackfoot
COUNSELOR

Vivian Ayoungman

WOULD YOU TELL ME OF YOUR CHILDHOOD?

I was born on the Blackfoot Indian Reserve, Gleichen, Alberta Canada. I attended an Anglican boarding School, called the Old Sun. It was named after a Blackfoot Chief. I started school at the age of seven and did not speak a word of English. Somehow I managed to make it to the 7th grade, at which time I was bussed to a nearby public school. It was tramatic. My cousin and I were the only Indians in our class. One thing I found out was that I had a poor self-image, but I soon found out that I could do just as well, even better than the non-Indians. My cousin and I were near the top of the class. Some of the students seem to resent that we did so well. We became quite competitive.

WHAT WERE SOME OF YOUR INTERESTS?

The Indian students were sort of left to themselves. There was little mixing at recess or lunch time. I tried to, and did get the top marks in the class. I remember attending a lot of rodeos, and the Sun Dance ceremony. We went to a lot of pow-wows. Coming from a ranching family, I spend a lot of time picking berries. We had our farm chores to do as well. I had to feed chickens, collect eggs, and look after the garden.

WHAT DO YOU REMEMBER OF FAMILY LIFE?

My grandmother used to come and visit us. She did not speak a word of English. She used to tell us a lot of the Indian Legends. We used to fight to get to sleep with her. We could listen to the stories over and over again. We only went home on week-ends from the boarding school. Vacations were spent at home. We were very close as a family. In those days there was no such thing as a baby sitter. We all went together as a family. I have five brothers and four sisters. Most of them are working on the reserve and two of them are working off the reserve. I went to high school in the City of Calgary where I stayed in a boarding home with a non-Indian family.

WHAT PERSONS MOST INFLUENCED YOU?

My parents were the main force in my life. They really supported us. I went home every week-end, and they drove us back to Calgary every Sunday so I never lost touch with the Reserve. I always knew I was going on to the university, because our parents encouraged me. I am grateful that my teachers recognized my potential. They helped me along, but I do remember that I didn't get any real guidance as to the vocation I should pursue. I recall in the 12th grade, staying awake nights wondering about what field I would go into. In the end I chose education.

From high school I enrolled in the University of Calgary. I took secondary education, with an emphasis in French. I was interested in the field on linguistics. I had some difficulty in narrowing my field to one area, there were so many things to do. While I was there I became a member of the International Students Association. This exposed me to many different cultures. It made me appreciate the diversity, the many life-styles, and the many different contributions that the different people have to offer. I also belonged to the Civil Liberties Association on campus. It helped to know that there were people behind you, people who would support you when you stand up for your rights. I really appreciated my whole university experience, because I gained a lot of confidence. It made me more outgoing, I was able to share my ideas with anybody. It was at this time I started to do a lot of public speaking. I became a kind of ambassador of good-will. The texts, the press, the content of so many school subjects either left out the Indian people, or gave a negative image. I spoke to youth clubs, ladies groups, and visited different schools speaking to classes. I remember being invited to political rallies. A highlight in my third year at the university was being asked by several Indian people to run for the "Indian Princess" title. I first won the Indian Princess of Calgary, then of Alberta, and then of Canada. That was in 1968. This made my speaking engagements more official, in a role of "ambassador of good-will."

WHAT KIND OF HOPES DO YOU HAVE FOR THE INDIAN PEOPLE?

For all people, I won't limit it to Indian people, I would like to see them get as much out of life as they can. I think an education provides them with this opportunity.

Formal education can open all kinds of doors for them. It provides them with an opportunity to make choices. An education may train you for a vocation, the concept is much wider. I like to learn new things. I really like challenges. Education helps you learn how to learn. So much of what I know does not come from my formal schooling. Instead of taking things for granted, I have become alert to the things I can learn from my family, the people around me, and the community.

WHAT HOPES DO YOU HAVE FOR YOUR OWN FUTURE?

I have had three years of teaching experience, and two years of counseling. With my training I feel I have a lot to offer in the field of Indian Education. There is a need for Indian people to work in curriculum development as consultants for non-Indian teachers, in counseling especially for the adult population which is almost non-existant across Canada, or in administration. I am a board member of the Old Sun Community College, which has only eight members. I was elected in 1974. There are about 125 full-time students at the present time. There are many evening classes and short-term workshops. This is a small college, struggling to survive, and get on its feet. The college is supported by the federal government. I think all of the students are Indian, mostly local residents. At the time they started the college I was working as a teacher at the Morley Indian School. When I transferred to the University of Calgary as a counselor I was closer to home, so I got more involved in what was going on in the Reserve. People asked me to run for Board of Directors of the Community College, and I was one of eight elected. The college has a lot of potential. At first the emphasis was on cultural education. It was also involved in high school completion programs. Later the college moved into vocational areas, such as farm maintainance, welding, secretarial training and the life skills program. Hobbies, enrichment programs, and academic upgrading and university extension classes are all in the plans for the next year.

WHAT MAJOR OBSTACLES DO YOU FEEL YOU HAVE OVERCOME?

I would not want to kid myself, or anyone else that things have just gone smoothly. Any young person goes through many choices and dilemmas. For example, just being able to stay in school with so many obstacles was extremely difficult. Being the only Indian in the Junior High, made it difficult to go to school each day. In the winter time, we prayed for a blizzard, so the buses wouldn't run. I was financed throughout by the Department of Indian Affairs, however, that did not eliminate financial hardships. Although I encountered problems, I never seriously considered dropping out of school.

ANY SUGGESTIONS FOR YOUNG INDIAN PEOPLE?

I would encourage young Indian people to obtain a formal education. It helps them to have more choices. At the same time, they must also retain their Indian language, their Indian values and other cultural traits. These do not need to clash. They enhance each other.

Roger Tsabetsye

Zuni
ARTIST

Roger Tsabetsye

I am very interested in the political and social conditions of the American Indian on the reservation. We cannot depend on the romanticism of the Indian today. I want the Indian to be in partnership with the rest of society. I would like the Indian to be self-sustaining. For too long we have been wards of the Federal government, and in most cases it is hard to break away from the way of life encouraged by the Bureau of Indian Affairs.

HOW DID YOU BEGIN YOUR ART WORK?

I attended government schools most of my life. I went to school in Zuni, New Mexico. In my growing up days, I did not know what I wanted in life. As I reflect on my early life, I was brought up in Catholic schools, which did not necessarily help me find myself -- who I really am as an artist.

I went to boarding school, where my dominant role in art and literature has opened a broad scope to the realities of life. Rather than making diagrams, and the proper use of English language, I wanted to identify myself as an Indian, a Zuni, with English as a second language. I think that has been a fault of Indian schools. Indians come from different tribes, and have different language patterns of their own. The language may not reflect the intelligence of the Indian.

I work in different media, painting, ceramics, silver. I studied for three years at the Rochester Institute of Technology. It was in the School of American Craftsmen, where I majored in silver and metal processing. I think that, as a creative artist, I did not find academics my bag. As a creative individual I approach things more from the conceiving a problem directly to the state where it can be conceived in the mind. I like to illustrate that experience.

Rather than trying to evolve a work from a book, I like to get myself directly involved with the subject. From the artistic point of view it is conceived in my mind. In most cases, what we can conceive in the mind can be illustrated by an artist with his hands.

WHAT MEDIA DO YOU MOST ENJOY?

Painting and ceramics, I think you can do almost anything with. You can create an experience, mood, color, and go back and work at it until you like it. There is no concept of time in the media of painting. Ultimately, in the media of painting, you can come through with a visual language of its own.

TELL ME ABOUT YOUR CHILDHOOD.

I was born on the Zuni reservation. There are two of us boys, and I have six sisters. I was always getting into mischief. In Zuni, most of our people are shepherds. They have sheep ranches. In the summer I was expected to herd the sheep on the ranch. It was about 15 miles from the village of Zuni.

Generally, during the summer season, the lambs were born. In those days we would find men from the village camped out. They would take those chores. There are several age groups. You could be sitting with a sixty-five year old man smoking bull-durham. It was initiation into manhood. There was always some kind of entertainment. There were games and dances. Wherever the men gathered there was activity. I used to stay with an eighty-year-old-man, a sort of philosopher. We called him "Dead Horse." We would teach him bad English. This was entertainment for those long nights and days. During the day you could sit under the trees, and he would tell you of the wonderment of nature. He would anticipate that in ten or twenty years the population explosion would occur, and we would have to go out into the White Man's world, and learn all the bad habits. He would tell us things that were coming, but not a special time. It was most intriguing and delightful. I cannot deny his vision and am living that experience.

WOULD YOU TELL ME OF THE CONSIGNMENT YOU DID FOR PRESIDENT LYNDON JOHNSON?

I was asked by President Johnson to do a squash blossom, typical of the south west, for the President of Costa Rica, in 1965. I was still at Rochester. It was part of the initiation of the War on Poverty. I was in Washington, D.C. during some of the conferences. I attended as a student from New York State, being an Indian representative. President Johnson was a practical man, down to earth, with a lot of common sense. He did one thing that will be remembered -- the War on Poverty projects. It recognized a lot of minority races, and especially the American Indians. Without that, we would not have the Indian self-determination programs we have.

85

DO YOU HAVE A FAMILY?

I have three children. One wife! Two boys and one girl. They are artistic, too. My upbringing was pretty strict. I was going to be a sheep-herder like my father. I don't try to dictate to my kids, as long as they stay out of trouble.

In 1975 I ran for tribal Governor, but was defeated. I may run again. In 1962 I was attending the former Sante Fe Indian School, now the Institute of American Indian Art. Lloyd Kiva was a major founder of the Institute, a Cherokee. Dr. Ballard, Fritz Scholder, and I were the first to implement the Institute, I helped set up the curriculum and the philosophy of the school. I taught in the Art Department, and was a student. I taught silversmithing. I was a student of the top artist-craftsmen of this country, showing in Japan and Europe.

I have shown at the Heard Museum, Phoenix, and the Scottsdale Indian National Art Show, as well as the Museum of Sante Fe. I have shown my jewelry and paintings at the New York American Indian Art Center.

I think it is becoming more and more evident that the Indian Youth and outlook on life will bring more participation. Rather than destroying traditions, they can build upon those traditions for a more vibrant and dynamic culture of their own. We can build upon past civilizations and great cultures for the Indian people.

Yvonne Talachy

Cochiti/Laguna
CRAFTSWOMAN

Yvonne Talachy

I was born one of two children in Sante Fe, New Mexico. In order that my father could continue his schooling, I was sent back to the Reservation to stay with my Grandparents, Herbert and Lillian Paisano. It was the Laguna Reservation. My mother is of the Laguna tribe; I am registered as a Cochiti.

I remember my early school days as troubled. The Indians were the only people I knew, being brought up on the Reservation. It was like being thrown into a lions den. It was hard to adjust. By then my Mother, was a receptionist for the Museum, the folk art museum in Sante Fe. My father was then with the State Dept. of Education and did a lot of traveling. He worked for the city public schools, and tried to coordinate between the Indian children and the state.

My father attended the Sante Fe Indian School, and got his college degree at the University of New Mexico. My brother stayed with my father's grandparents at Cochiti Pueblo while I stayed at Laguna.

WHAT WERE YOUR INTERESTS AS A CHILD?

I was a loner. My interest was doll collecting. My parents would get me dolls from overseas. I still have them to this day. I picked up skiing in elementary school; I entertained myself with music. I played clarinet, flute, and piano. I still continue with my music, and like every facet of music. I like to sing, but my vocal chords are not tuned in.

My childhood was unhappy because my folks had troubles. I think it has reflected on my life. I don't blame either one of them as they were trying to do the best for themselves and for us. But we were neglected. They were helping thousands of other people promoting education. They were finding new ways to incorporate a young person's continuance of education, self-determination. I remember my father giving talks to the schools. I felt I could have used the time from my folks.

Right now I am a silversmith, and I attend night classes at Espanola Vocational-Technical School, Espanola, New Mexico. I figure as a safety measure I have accounting as a skill to fall back on. My silversmithing is a source of income. I sell for Navajo Mountain Indian Arts and Crafts, Los Alamos, New Mexico. I work in all facets of public relations, and I'm learning the retail business.

WHAT ARE SOME OF YOUR DREAMS?

One of my dreams is to be happy within myself. And until I can find that time, whether it be now or later, I eventually want to go into education. I enjoy the business experience and enjoy meeting people.

There are so many areas I want to get into; I don't just want to leave it at one thing. There is such a vast range of ideas that interest me. I have been at silversmithing a year. I never thought I could do so well with silversmithing. When I do my silversmith work it is important that I do work from my own feeling. It is hard for me to do something that is someone else's idea. Their idea of beauty is not necessarily beautiful to me.

What I want to do is my creation, my love, my expression of feeling. That is what I want to do. This is my first year in college. I find I have so many interests. I think in each interest I want to develop what talent I have.

WHAT DO YOU HAVE TO SAY ABOUT THE FUTURE OF NATIVE AMERICANS?

It is very hard to generalize. There are so many needs that are yet to be met. Every day new problems arise. You have to handle each problem the best you can, whether it be in the schools or home. My children are in elementary school. I have two children and do all I can to help them. I am on the Parent-Teachers Committee in San Juan Pueblo. I have worked in Head-Start programs. I help them get on their feet, and find and meet the needs of small children. I have worked with the Crafts Cooperative in San Juan, OKE-OWEENCE. I joined as a member a year before I was elected President of the Crafts Cooperative. I worked to get it on its feet. We sought the help of the eight Northern Pueblos. We wrote proposals for moneys to bring in resources for the artisans. We got grants from the Four Corners Regional Area Foundation. We incorporated skill training into the cooperative to train young people in the arts and crafts of that particular pueblo.

The other success I had while working with the Coop was assembling the NATIVE AMERICAN COOKBOOK, published by a Chicago firm. I think the most success I had was working with the people and helping them learn to cooperate . . My concern was to keep them happy and to learn to work together. Without them there would be no cooperative. There was much dissension when I came into the Coop.

My main concern now is seeing how the craftsman can benefit from his creations, his work. I want to see that the manufacturing business does not hurt the Indian craftsman. Right now, with all the factory stuff, the Indian craftsman is competing with his own people, plus the white man, too. It is a continual war, and dealers often find loopholes. The Indian must do all in his power to see that Indian arts are maintained.

I wish the Indian could rise above all common problems, and come to one objective, "AN INDIAN IN ONE!" I hope that the Pueblos, and all Native Americans can work together and see that they have common interests. Until they realize you are one kind of Indian, and I am one kind of Indian, there will be conflict.

I hope for my children, and all children, a good education. I hope parents can instill the importance of education. I think it is important to educate the parents, too. Without their help, a child is helpless; they are not grown up enough to make use of their lives. By screaming at them, yelling at them, beating them, this is not the way to go about it.

I hope I can make my children happy and that they can live happy lives. I believe if I am happy they will be happy.

Louis Tewanima

Hopi
TRACK CHAMPION

Louis Tewanima

"What do you want a track suit for?" asked coach Glenn "Pop" Warner, the famous coach of the Carlisle Indian School, Carlisle, Pennsylvania.

"Me run fast good," Tewanima is supposed to have answered, "All Hopis run Fast!"

Louis Tewanima, who came from Shongopovi, Second Mesa of the Hopi tribe weighed only 110 pounds, but Warner found that Louis ran like a deer. After that visit with "Pop" Warner, Tewanima cleaned up everything that America had to offer in the 10 and 15-mile races. "Pop" Warner continued:

"Once I took him to New York for a 10-mile competition in Madison Square Garden, and after he looked at the track, he turned to me and said: 'Me afraid get mixed up go round and round. You tell me front man and I get him.' "

"About the middle of the race I managed to catch his eye and point out the runners who led him, and one by one he picked them up, finally finishing in a burst of speed that established a new world's record."

Jim Thorpe, the Sac and Fox triple threat Indian, remembered his teammate in 1940 stating:

"I recall the day Carlisle had a dual meet with Lafayette College. They had 20 men on their track team. We had only three Indians, Frank Mount Pleasant, Louis Tewanima, and myself."

"A big crowd turned out for the meet. Mount Pleasant and I won the sprints. Tewanima and I took the middle-distance events. And I was lucky enough to win most of the field contests. THE THREE OF US LICKED LAFAYETTE."

Then later, Tewanima, Thorpe and Mount Pleasant triumphed over a strong Syracuse University team in another dual meet. Tewanima and Thorpe were so good in track, in fact, that both were selected for the Olympic team without having to undergo trials -- a really rare honor.

PHOENIX SPORTS AWARD

In 1957, Tewanima, the Olympic Medal Winner, received a standing ovation at the Phoenix Sports Award dinner at which he was the first person inducted into the Arizona Sports Hall of Fame. He described how in his childhood he and his friends from the Hopi mesa would run down jackrabbits for the fun of it.

Occasionally Tewanima would run down to Winslow, Arizona and back--120 miles round-trip--just to watch the trains go by.

OFF TO OLYMPICS

On June 14, 1912, Tewanima and Jim Thorpe were among the 164 Olympians--whose ranks included famed Hawaiian swimmer Duke Kahanamoku--who sailed for Stockholm, Sweden. Earlier, Tewanima had competed in the Marathon in the 1908 Olympics in London, but he was a novice at the 26-mile distance and wound up ninth among the 58 starters, fewer than half of whom finished.

At Stockholm, the story was different. Although the Flying Finn, Kannes Kolehmainen, the greatest distance runner the world had seen up to then, finished first in the grueling 10,000-meter race, Tewanima came in second.

However, his performance at the Olympics in Sweden was so fast that for 52 years it remained the best time any American ever attained in that event. U.S. Marine Billy Mills eclipsed Tewanima's record at Tokyo in 1964.

"Pop" Warner and Tewanima returned home together. And after a month back at Carlisle Indian School, Tewanima decided to return to his Second Mesa, and the Hopi people--to tend his sheep and raise his crops.

It was in 1954 that Arizona newscaster and sports-reporter Bill Close of KOOL-TV in Phoenix accompanied Louis Tewanima to New York City, where he was named to the All-Time United States Olympic Track and Field Team. Says an editorial in the Arizona Republic, "Louis Tewanima was truly a man of his land and his people. Despite his estimated 90-some years, Tewanima-- who together with Jim Thorpe and a handful of other Indians led Carlisle Indian School to its greatest moment in track glory-- did not die of old age. A religious man throughout his life, he fell from a steep cliff after losing his way while returning from a Hopi religious ceremoney at the Kiva a mile from his home."

Bill Close remembered taking Louis Tewanima around Manhattan Island, New York. He took him atop the Empire State Building and while the Hopi athlete was impressed with the height, his reaction in surveying the asphalt jungle below was, "No grass for sheep." Tewanima returned to his Second Mesa to live out his life among the Hopi people whom he loved. The famed Hopi runner is a link with a historic past.

Jim Thorpe

Sac and Fox
"WORLD'S GREATEST ATHLETE"

Jim Thorpe

"The Greatest Athlete in the World" is the way King Gustav of Sweden described James Francis Thorpe, better known as "Jim Thorpe." The King of Sweden was referring to America's greatest all-round athlete, a champion at football, track and a baseball star. Jim Thorpe was one of the products of the famous "Pop" Warner coach at Carlisle Indian School in Pennsylvania.

James Francis Thorpe was a Sac and Fox Indian born in Prague, Oklahoma on May 28, 1888. He played football at Carlisle Indian School in 1907 and 1908 and left school to play baseball with the Fayetteville and Rocky Mount Teams of the Eastern Carolina League for $15 a week. Then he returned to Carlisle in 1911. In one of the greatest football spectaculars of all time, he scored a touchdown and kicked field goals of 23, 45, 37, and 48 yards as Carlisle defeated Harvard College 18 to 15. It was in 1912 he scored 25 touchdowns and 198 points for Carlisle, an all-time record.

In 1912 at the Olympic Games in Sweden he won the decathalon and pentathlon. But it was his playing professionally for a summer baseball team that cost him his Olympic medals. Following the Olympics when it was learned by a newspaper reporter that Thorpe had received money for playing baseball, he had to return his Olympic prizes.

It was in baseball that Thorpe played in the outfield for the New York Giants, then for the Cincinnati Reds and next he played for the Boston Braves. He played professionally from 1913 through 1919, batting .252 in 289 games.

Jim Thorpe played professional football for Canton, Cleveland, for the Oorang Indians from Marion, Ohio, Toledo, Rock Island and for the New York Giants. He made his last appearance in football with the Chicago Cardinals in 1929.

Thorpe became the first president of the American Professional Football Association in 1920. It was in 1950 Thorpe was voted the best athlete of the first half of the Century by the powerful Associated Press in a poll. He has been named to both the college and to the professional football halls of fame.

Michael Curtez, the noted film director chose to team up with Warner Brothers and in 1949 made a feature film of the world famous athlete, Jim Thorpe. Roger Axford, Dean of the Faculty at Bacone at the time, recalls Warner Brothers taking over the campus at Bacone College, Muskogee, Oklahoma, which became overnight "Carlisle Indian School."

Burt Lancaster became Jim Thorpe, Phyllis Thaxter became Thorpe's childhood sweetheart and actor Bickford became the famous "Pop" Warner for the film. JIM THORPE--ALL AMERI-CAN became the feature length film, with the real Jim Thorpe acting as an advisor. Many of the Bacone College Indian students were paid as extras. The College was all but at a stand-still for three weeks, but what better way to teaching a drama class? And Michael Curtez, the Austrian refugee film director was made an honorary member of the faculty. The tragedies of a "mixed-marriage" and of Jim Thorpe's struggle with success in the Olympics and his battle against drink were all realistically portrayed.

"I hope I will be partly excused by the fact that I was simply an Indian schoolboy and I did not know all about such things." wrote Jim Thorpe in a letter to the Amateur Athletic Union, following accusations that he had violated his amateur standing and must return the Olympic medals. No one, especially Thorpe, could have foreseen the sudden and tragic decline of his athletic fortunes. It was while Thorpe was practicing baseball at Worchester and enjoying the attention of children and reporters alike that he was spotted by Charley Glancy, a former coach at Rocky Mount. Mr. Glancy mentioned to Roy Johnson, a reporter with the Worchester TELEGRAM, that he had coached Thorpe several years ago in the semi-pro league.

Dr. Michael D. Koehler, a grandson of Jim Thorpe and a leading educator, writes "A closer examination of historical data reveals two interesting elements of Thorpe's pre-Olympic athletic career. As was the case with all the Indians at schools like Carlisle and Haskell, Thorpe and the other athletes had to request from their agents back home increases in their normal allotments for clothing needs or special occasions.

Because so many of the Indians, especially the athletes, were in their late teens or well into their twenties during their tenure at Carlisle, the ongoing financial dependency they experienced became more and more distasteful to them with each passing season. That explains why, when Thorpe left Carlisle to play at Rocky Mount, no one at the school expected him to return. It also may explain the reason why he used his real name for the team roster, because many used fictitious names. Thorpe doubt-lessly expected his experience at Rocky Mount to supplement his agency income, thereby allaying much of his financial dependency. Certainly he expected it to be a first step toward a career in the major leagues, which, ironically it was to become."

It is certainly true that Jim Thorpe is made of the stuff from which legends are made. Jim's brother had died when very young, some say from malnutrition. Jim's early home life had been characterized by poverty and general insecurity, living among the Sac and Fox tribe. Thorpe became a disciplined and talented athlete, a triple threat, as they call it in the world of sports.

Two senators in the United States Senate have taken an interest in the Jim Thorpe legacy. Senator Burdick of South Dakota and Senator Percy of Illinois have asked that Jim Thorpe's amateur status during the years 1901 through 1912 be "re-evaluated." Again the nation and the world is being given the opportunity to forgive Thorpe and to acknowledge officially his reputation as one of the world's greatest athletes. Two prestigious organizations are seeking the reinstatement of Thorpe's amateur status-- The United States Olympic Committee and the Amateur Athletic Union. The ultimate decision must, however, be made by the International Olympic Committee.

Among the many private persons who have made an appeal by letter to the IOC in Switzerland, perhaps the most significant is that of President Gerald Ford, who wrote: "I hope the Committee will consider this request and act with a sense of equity in the light of history and of the contribution that Jim Thorpe has made to the world of sport."

The Oxford Companion to World Sports and Game says that James Francis Thorpe "American athlete, was perhaps the most versatile in history." Fortunately, Jim Thorpe's three daughters, Grace, Charlotte and Gail are actively promoting the Indian cause and working to vindicate the name and restore the honors to Jim Thorpe--All American.

Jim Thorpe died at his home in Lomita, California on March 28, 1953. A Pennsylvania town, JIM THORPE, formerly Mauch Chunk, was named for him in 1954. Many Americans are working for Thorpe's amateur standing to be restored. He has been punished too long already!

Dr. Richard West

Cheyenne/Arapaho
PAINTER

Dr. Richard West

"He shoots a straight arrow" was my observation as I watched Dick West stretch his bow and struck a bullseye on the target against the tree. Dick West is one of the most handsome men I have known and stands close to six foot four inches tall. He has wavy jet black hair and a winning smile. His piercing eyes sparkle when he tells you a story and he loves to kid his friends.

Dr. Walter Richard West, best known as Dick was the Director of the Art Department at Bacone College, Muskogee, when I knew him. He was dedicated to the education of Indian youth and worked in oils, watercolor, wood carving and metals. A talented artist, he brought the best out in his students, working patiently with each young budding artist.

I remember taking Dick and two Hopi artists, Burt Preston of Hotevilla, Arizona and Vernon Russell from Bacabi, Arizona to the Philbrook Art Museum in Tulsa for an evening of painting. The Bacone artists headed by Dick West made a sketch of their two dimensional painting and then did the painting from beginning to the finish. In exchange the Art League of Tulsa brought their ten artists to our college gym at Bacone and before more than 300 completed their paintings and the ten lucky persons who had the right number got a finished painting at the end of the evening. What an exciting evening. What an exciting method to promote the arts. And that illustrates the imagination and leadership of Dick West.

Dick and Mary West lived in a log cabin on the campus circle. They had two lively boys, Richard Jr. and Jimmy. I understand one of the boys is a physician in Oklahoma now. But then, the boys played cowboys and Indians on the college campus. I recall vividly the president's son Willard Thompson, always wanted to be the Indian and the West boys wanted to play the part of the cowboys. Ironic humor, I kept telling myself.

Mary West was an accomplished musician. A more devoted wife no man has had. Mary adored Dick and always beamed in his presence. Mary stood about five foot six and when strapping Dick stood his full six-four they looked like Mutt and Jeff. We had many a fun evening eating popcorn and singing with the Wests for they were fun people. Mary played the piano for the Bacone Singing Redmen until she contracted a brain tumor which incapacitated her for some time and finally took her life.

I can visualize the house the West's lived in. They lived in what had at one time been the home economics demonstration house. Out in front of the house was a large iron kettle that had at one time been used to teach the native Indian girls to cook in the open and by the most primitive methods. But it was the Baptist missionaries purpose to prepare them to live in their reservation environment and to live a more full life.

Each Christmas we look forward to receiving the Christmas card from the West family. Dick is now famous for his ability to depict the religious motif in his paintings. He often shows Christ as an Indian and is noted for his painting of the nativity scene, with the manger scene in Indian dress, including the shepherds.

Dick West was born at Dalington, Oklahoma, September 8, 1912. He attended the Concho Indian School, took his high school at Haskell Institute in Kansas and completed Bacone Junior College, Muskogee, Oklahoma where he returned to teach most of his professional career. Dick received Bachelor of Fine Arts and Master of Fine Arts from University of Oklahoma. He has also attended University of Redlands and Tulsa University.

Dick was honored with an Honorary Doctor of Humane Letters from Eastern Baptist College in 1963. He was voted the Outstanding Cheyenne of the Year in 1968. He appears in Who's Who in American Art; Who's Who in the South and Southwest; Who's Who in Oklahoma; American Indian Painters and Personalities of the South.

The thing I remember about Dick is that he liked to "pull my leg". He loved a joke and has a delightful sense of humor. He never took himself too seriously and was impatient with folks who did. I was serving as Dean of Bacone College, and my wife Geri was teaching Religious Education when we worked with the Wests. Whenever we had disciplinary problems (and I got many students out of jail for drinking while I was at the College) Dick could give me advise and insight that was priceless. He helped me understand "Indian time" he called it, the discipline of permissiveness of many of the tribes and an understanding of the cultural shock many of the Indian students experienced in trying to adjust to the "folk-ways" of the White man. I remember we had a great grand-daughter of Geranimo, Napanee Grayhorse, as a student and the daughter of the publisher of the Cherokee language newspaper, Delores, a bright, talented girl.

Says Burt Preston, Tuba City Hopi artist who studied for three years with Dick West, "Dick I remember as a friend. I also remember him as an individual who played a role of a godfather. The reason why I thought of him as a godfather is because Dick shared his life experiences with me, his intimate thoughts about his early life as well as his present and future expectations for me as an artist and as an individual."

"He told me about the problems of adjusting to non-Indian life. He told me at one time that an Indian starts out in life with already a strike against him, and that an Indian has to strive harder than the non-Indian. He said that if an Indian could prove himself, he is just as capable of being accepted as any member of his community."

"I think Dick is truely a friend of the Indian students. This was gained through the experience of working in other settings besides Bacone. He was a teacher with the Bureau of Indian Affairs before going to Bacone. He was interested in athletics, was an outstanding football player, and, I think, coached at Phoenix Indian School."

"I visited Dick at Bacone in 1964 and he showed me his gown from the honorary doctorate he received from a University in Pennsylvania. He was proud of it. He called me "Son". That was the kind of relationship we had."

"Dick inspired me to pursue a career in the field of art. He said that I had potential not only in art, but in whatever field I wanted to go into. He encouraged me to get a degree in art and fall back on that so that I would really be happy. He knew that art is my first love. Dick inspired me both through bull-sessions and discussions of outstanding artists and their techniques."

Dick attempted to preserve the Indian culture through his art, the Indian dances and he was involved in the formation of the Indian Club. He did the sign language for the Singing Redmen. He also instructed Al Douglas, an Eastern Indian in sign language, especially in the Lord's Prayer. The Redmen performed all over the United States.

Dick has nurtured many young artists like Burt Preston. His products are teaching and painting throughout the United States, so his influence is felt far and wide.

Dick has received three grand prizes. He received the Waite Phillips Award and a trophy from the Philbrook Art Center. He is known for his traditional Indian paintings as well as for his portraits. He paints abstractions now and utilizes other European-derived art styles.

Dick West is now the Director of Art at the Haskell Indian Institute, a Junior College in Lawrence, Kansas. He continues to hunt with bow and arrow and portrays his love of nature in his sensitive paintings.

Gay Lawrence

Sioux

Gay Lawrence

As Gay Lawrence grew up on the Cheyenne River Sioux Reservation in South Dakota, she was surrounded by much family love and natural beauty that were to be influences on her throughout her entire life. She describes her life there as a child as being "free and happy".

"My early life was spent in Cheyenne Agency, a beautiful town with wild rose bushes fringed by forest. We were boarded on one side by the Missouri River and on the other side by prairie grasslands. My parents, Violet and Augustus Kingman, were of French and Indian extraction."

Gay was an only child, but because her mother was a dorm matron for the little boys, she grew up with 40 to 50 "brothers". "My first thirteen years were spent in this setting, with this influence, and surrounded by all the love and peace an extended Indian family could have."

During her childhood Gay also learned much about her Indian heritage, especially from her father. She is a Miniconjous Sioux, a name that means "those who plant by the stream" in the Dakota language. Gay's father was a Wicasas Yatapikas, a part of the supreme group of counselors of the Sioux nation who acted as the tribe's executives when the tribe came together. In order for a man to become a Wicasas Yatapikas, he had to be considered wise, generous, compassionate and strong. The famous Sioux leader Crazy Horse had been a Wicasas.

Gay's father was a person who possessed the qualities of the Wicasas and practiced them in his daily living. He set a good example for Gay to follow in what it meant to be Indian. Gay speaks with great respect of her father, "I guess the person who has had the greatest impact on me is my father. He practices what he preaches. He is very Indian, and I was raised by him to be Indian. He does not drink or smoke, is a very fine person, and was always there when I needed him."

When Gay graduated from eighth grade, her parents sent her to a Catholic girls' school in Aberdeen, South Dakota. They hoped that it would "overcome my tomboyishness and give me opportunities I would otherwise not have." Compared to her free and relaxed way of growing up, the school was very rigid and structured, and the "foreign environment was a shock--culturally, socially, educationally and emotionally." During this time, though, she was influenced by Sister Marie. Gay says, "She was the music teacher. She was always after me to practice my piano. She made me cut my fingernails. She helped me because she felt I had talent. She encouraged me to compete and to have recitals." Because of her influence, Gay went on to win many honors in music during her high school and college years.

Gay's family had always expected her to go on to college, and since Gay had always enjoyed working with people, she went into elementary education with minors in music and English. In addition to completing her education, she also married and had two sons during her college years.

Gay's first teaching assignment was with the Bureau of Indian Affairs on the Pine Ridge Reservation at the Oglala Community School. Not only did the students come during the day, but there were many students who boarded there, so the teachers lived on the campus and participated in many of the activities with their students. "We taught during the day and were swept up in the after-school activities which dealt with trying to keep the boarding school students busy and provide them with a family living environment. I spent three happy years at Oglala Community School."

It was during this time that Gay learned how desperate many young people are for attention and acceptance. Many parents were not there when their children needed them, as her father always had been for her. Gay sensed that "the personal touch was so important. We had students who would hang around and offer to clean blackboards just to stay around." She participated in many of their clubs and activities and also helped provide the family love and environment that the boarding students needed. "I remember many times helping patch knees for the numerous little boys' jeans and stitching seams in the little girls' dresses."

From Pine Ridge, Gay was transferred to her home reservation to a similar school setting at Cheyenne Eagle Butte, South Dakota. Here, though, the reservation was not a closed reservation, so many of her students were non-Indians from the town. Again Gay was involved in many community-school activities. While the teachers only had to contribute what time they wanted to outside activities, Gay always gave many of her hours after school to making the life of the children more fun and meaningful. She remembers, "assisting the matron in an evening of fine-combing heads for lice; the children made the best of the event by making a game of the whole business."

After her two years at Eagle Butte, Gay moved to Spearfish, South Dakota and spent two years there. During that time she did part-time teaching for Black Hills State College and substitute teaching for the public schools. This was followed by six months in Washington D.C. where she worked in a large department store.

A new experience awaited Gay when the family moved from Washington to Minneapolis, Minnesota, and she began work in an inner-city school. "My students consisted of wealthy Whites, who were bussed in from the suburbs, Blacks, Indians, poor

105

Whites and some Mexicans. I enjoyed the challenge of the neighborhood and diverse student population." While she was there, she was elected by the parents to the Community Education Board. This board helped bring education to the neighborhood when they hired a Community School Coordinator and organized social and educational activities and programs that were offered to the public at the school after the regular school days. Always active, Gay spent two very busy years in Minneapolis before moving to Bismarck, North Dakota.

In Bismarck, Gay accepted a position with the United Tribes Employment Training Center as Supervisor of the Personal Development Department. United Tribes is an Indian Corporation formed by an alliance of five tribes, and they contract with the Bureau of Indian Affairs for financing to operate programs such as vocational training, curriculum development, and prison parole programs. Here Gay's department was involved with assisting adults in personal development. They offered classes in resume writing, effective interviewing, taxes and budgeting, consumer information and Indian culture as well as GED programs. Gay feels strongly that "it is important to train people not only in academics but in personal development."

After four months in this position, Gay was asked to plan and open an elementary school at the United Tribes Employment Training Center which would be for the children of the staff and the trainees. After the long and difficult task of organizing the school, grades 1-6 were opened with Gay as the new principal. Six months later the facilities were enlarged and two more grades were added. "We had a unique situation. The staff was all Indian except for two teachers and one Black aide. The students came from Indian tribes all over the United States. Their parents were from low socio-economic backgrounds and were themselves being trained in a vocation on the same campus." During this time Gay also submitted a proposal that was funded which started a Community Education Program at U.T.E.T.C. Activities expanded to include a night program that rivaled the day program for keeping everyone busy. Tribal members learned each others' songs, dances and traditions. There were classes in cooking, beadwork, auto mechanics, photography and much more. Gay found it difficult to leave the thriving campus when her husband began working in Phoenix for the Bureau of Indian Affairs Area Office in Education. Never one to be idle, Gay began work as Title IV Coordinator for Indian Education for the Scottsdale, Arizona Public School System.

"Throughout my life, as I have worked and lived, I have tried to keep my Indian values preeminently in mind. I have learned considerably from all my experiences and have tried to contribute as much as I have acquired." Those Wicasas qualities, which her father possessed and passed on to her, have enabled Gay to contribute greatly to all those who have been touched by her involvement and work.

Carol Allen Weston

Quapaw/Euchee/Cherokee
RECREATION SPECIALIST

Carol Allen Weston

WHAT DO YOU REMEMBER OF YOUR CHILDHOOD?

"Well, we moved a lot. My earliest recollection is when my father graduated from high school. He graduated from high school at Quapaw, Oklahoma. I also remember being at his college graduation. I was about four at the time. He went to Wichita, Kansas. From there we lived in Oklahoma, until my father got his break at New Mexico University. I started getting my training in dancing, gymnastics, track and field, and swimming. It was a happy childhood. We are very close family. We did everything together. My father, Dr. Noah Allen is superintendent of the Phoenix Indian High School.

"My mother is a dedicated person. She made all our clothes for us, she worked all day, and then came home and cooked for us. She has always been a secretary. Mother is so talented, I have had other sisters say they would most like to be like her. She has sewed cheerleader uniforms, softball uniforms, and prom dresses. I have four sisters. Two graduated in physical education-recreation. The third is a senior, going to South Dakota State. She wants to be a professional tennis player. She can make it I think. My youngest sister is in grade school in Phoenix."

"It was at New Mexico State that I decided to be a physical education instructor. We had to wash the football helmets, line the football fields; we had to hold the tape for the track meets. My father didn't have any sons, so he made his daughters do the work that men would do. I started competing in track and field, and tennis when Dad went to the University of Oregon. My sister Pat and I decided we would train for the Olympics. My field was shot-put. We did this all through high school. As happens with all young girls, we had to decide between sports and men. I decided to take sports all through college. My sister decided to take men! I competed all over the West Coast in shotput, for Pacific University just outside Portland."

WHAT EVENT DO YOU REMEMBER BEST?

"I remember best winning the shotput in 1965 in the All Northwest Track and Field championships held at University of Oregon. We competed with women from Australia, New Zealand, and the United States. Then, we moved to Kansas. Unfortunately, Kansas did not have women's inter-collegiate sports in any way. As a result of this circumstance, I had to turn to officiating. I have a national rating, meaning I can officiate at any national competition in softball, basketball, and volleyball. I was most often the only Indian competing in women's inter-collegiate sports."

"I think I am most proud of the time I was elected a cheerleader at college - both at Wichita State and at Pacific University. I was a pom-pom girl at Wichita State University. My outlets were officiating and cheerleading. After graduation I decided that since women's sports weren't "big" at that time, I would go into dancing. I came to Arizona State University to get my Master of Science in physical education, and competed in 1970. I got a job at Haskell Indian Junior College teaching dance, and track and field. This was an exciting challenge because Indian women did not feel at ease in front of group, or running before a large crowd. We had drill teams, pom-pom dancing, modern dance, and I directed the cheerleaders. It grew from about six girls to nearly 75 girls in four years. I was really proud of this. Our track and field grew from zero to about 30 girls. We competed against major universities in Kansas."

"Haskell Junior College had a teacher reduction, and I had to go. They had hired too many temporary teachers. I found another vocation -- I was forced into it. I decided to become a Director of Student Activities. I got a job at Flandreau Indian High School in South Dakota. It is run by the Bureau of Indian Affairs. I was responsible for intermurals, all student organizations, and all social events. We had about 600 students from about 34 different tribes. I think I learned most from the experience, that every Indian tribe is different. But each Indian is a human being that has feelings. I had been an Oklahoma Indian, and I learned a lot about the northern plains Indians. One day, I received a call from the Phoenix office of the Bureau of Indian Affairs. They offered me a position as Deputy Federal Programs Administrator. They told me I could help more Indian students if I would accept the job. So, of course, I took the job. It is a federal post at a GS-12. I think that Title IX, which gives equal opportunity to women, had a major impact on their decision to hire me."

"A major influence in my life has been my father. He always expected top quality from us, not mediorcrity. He is the best educator I have ever met. The qualities I most admire is that he is generous with his time and money, and he is extremely honest. He has empathy for all human beings. When he does something he does it with all his energy. He is not a quiter."

ARE THERE ANY DIFFICULT TIMES YOU HAVE HAD IN LIFE?

"When I was at New Mexico State I set my goal to be a physical education instructor, and I had accomplished that by the time I was 23. I had to set a new goal. Actually, the greatest frustration is my size as a woman in a non-Indian society. In an Indian society the size of a woman has no bearing on her sex-appeal. The way I overcame this is to accept myself as I am, and not let other people's opinions make me sad. That is where I met my husband, in the Indian society. He accepted me the way I am. We met at Flandreau, South Dakota. He is in maintenance work. He is an older Indian man, who still believes in "old Indian ways." By this I mean he is patient, loving, and he listens very close to what I have to say. We have most in common our love of people. He is very accepting. He enjoys being with me, and we go together to Parent-Advisory meetings, Ttitle I meetings which consider public laws in relation to education, and to church. The church is very important in his life. Many of his family have been Episcopal ministers. That is in the Dakotas. He is a Santee-Sioux."

DO YOU REMEMBER YOUR GRANDPARENTS?

"Most of my Indian background culture has come from my Cherokee grandmother. I remember her singing to us when we were little, in Cherokee of course. I remember her disciplining us. We had to do something really bad before she would discipline us. Mostly with strong words. She would take us out in the woods to look for wild plants. She taught us to cook blackberry dumpling and, of course, fried bread. Her name is Lucy Daylight. She is about 90 years old now. She still lives in Oklahoma. Every year she looks forward to the grandchildren coming home, and taking her to the pow-wows, and Indian festivals. It is called Devil's Promenade, and is held at Quapaw. That is the only chance Indians have to get together, and that is their social life. You meet all your old friends there."

WHAT DO YOU HOPE FOR THE INDIAN PEOPLE?

"I hope they will accept every other tribe as their brother, and unite. For the young Indian I think the best thing they can do for themselves is set a high goal and go after it. Years ago young people wanted to be Chief, then Commissioner of Indian Affairs, and now they can be anything they want to be. I would urge young Indian people to get an education. They can then make a choice between the Indian culture and the non-Indian culture, or they can combine this and make their own life."

"I just want to continue to help the Indians in whatever way I can. I am now visiting Indian schools and see that educational services are provided, kindergarten through twelfth grade, for quality education. We recommend improved services to the Bureau of Indian Affairs, hoping that the Education Director will make the necessary changes. It may take me a while, but I have as a goal to get my doctorate, and to see how much I can do for Indian people before I die.''

Roxie Woods

Athapascan - Eskimo

AMERICAN WOMAN'S
DOG SLED CHAMPION

Roxie Woods

An exciting event for the state of Alaska is the North American Women's Dog Sled Race held at Nenana, Alaska in March. This year twelve women competed with their dog teams from all over the "49th state".

One of the leading women in Alaska now is Ms. Roxie Woods, four time winner of the race. She has disciplined both herself and her dogs to run the nearly fifteen miles in 35 minutes and 47.38 seconds. Many of the young women of Alaska dream of emulating her skill and fortitude.

The following is an interview with the Alaskan Champion with Roger W. Axford of Tempe, Arizona who was at Nenana and observed the races.

Axford - "Roxie, would you mind saying how it feels to be one of the winners in the race?"

Woods - "Feels fine."

Axford - "How do you attempt to keep the dogs in line?"

Woods - "Well, we start out first thing in the fall and start training them right away -- train them all winter."

Axford - "How many races have you won?"

Woods - "Oh, this year I won the women's world championship down in Anchorage and then the women's north american here in Nenana."

Axford - "How much was the prize down there?"

Woods - "750 dollars."

Axford - "How much does this one amount to?"

Woods - "Well, depends on how I did today, but there is $2,000 total in the purse and $4,050 on the whole race."

Axford - "Which ones of the dogs tends to be the most important, is it the lead dog?"

Woods - "Yes, you need a good lead dog."

Axford - "You're an Indian in background, right? I'm doing a book on Native Americans."

Woods - "Yes, I'm part Athapascan and part Eskimo, too."

Axford - Roxie says that she feeds the dogs herself and plays with them, pets them. She runs them about four or five times each week so that gives a chance for a very intimate relationship and friendship with the dogs. Right now she is taking the harnesses off the dogs.

Axford - "Roxie, will you tell me about where you were born?"

Woods - "I was born in Fairbanks, Alaska."

Axford - "How many in the family?"

Woods - "Seven sisters."

Axford - "Any brothers?"

Woods - "No."

Axford - "Your mother and daddy, are they still living?" "Where do they live?"

Woods - "Yes, well my Dad . . . . he's been racing dogs for the past 30 some years."

Axford - "Did he teach you some of this?"

Woods - "Yes, I learned alot from him, but mostly mushers have to learn on their own. Can't be told things -- from experience."

Axford - "Does it teach you independence?"

Woods - "I don't know."

Axford - "Resourcefulness?"

Woods - "It gives you a feeling of accomplishment when you see all the dogs working together."

Axford - "A lot of cooperation."

Woods - "A lot of hard work and time, too."

Axford - "Where did you go to school?"

Woods - "I went to school in Fairbanks and went to school outside (in the "lower 48" states) for two years."

Axford - "Where did you go?"

Woods - "Marysville and Edmonton, Washington. That's when I was little. I went to school for five years in Circle, it's a little town on the Yukon, and went one year in Sheldon and Jackson."

Axford - "One of your admirers? Oh is this your little girl?"

Woods - "Yes"

Axford - "What a sweetheart. How many children do you have?"

Woods - "Two, a little boy 8, and a little girl 6."

Axford - "What are their names?"

Woods - "Raymond and Tammy."

Axford - "How did you get into this racing?"

Woods - "My dad has been racing for a long time, and I started racing when I was about 16. I think this is the 10th North American Women's that I have run."

Axford - "Is that right, the tenth one?"

Woods - "Yes."

Axford - "Where were some of the others?"

Woods - "The Women's Northern American Sled Dog race in Fairbanks."

Axford - "Both men and women?"

Woods - "No women's. Then they have the Open North American which is traditionally called the men's race but it is open to both men and women."

Axford - "And did you participate?"

Woods - "Last year I ran in that -- that was the first time I ever ran in it, I came in 8th."

Axford - "Eight out of how many?"

Woods - "14, I think."

Axford - "What was the prize in that?"

Woods - "I don't know. They have usually on their open champ-ionships in Anchorage and Fairbanks around $10,000 total purse."

Axford - "What would you say for young people about raising dogs? Anything you would suggest?"

Woods - "I think it is a really good outlet because I think kids learn responsibility. They have to take care of the animals and it's a good way to get out and get exercise and you learn a lot from the dogs cause each one is an individual and you have to work with them, know them, and they have to have faith in you, too, or else they are not going to be working their best for you."

Axford - "What advice would you give young people today -- I'm doing this little book on Native Americans, and you are going to be one of those Indians. What advice would you give to young people today?"

Woods - "Well, no matter what you do, do your best, whether it is in education or being a housewife, or in sports, or whatever you are in. Always strive to do your best at whatever you do."

Axford - "Did you live in Rampart for awhile? Where did you meet your husband?"

Woods - "I met him in Fairbanks but we've been living in Rampart for the last two summers and then we lived there half this winter fishing and stuff in the summer."

Axford - "Fish for salmon?"

Woods - "Yes for our dogs and ourselves."

Axford - "My son has been doing that, too, up here in Nenana. That's why I'm up here. Well, I wish you every good thing for the future, and if anything comes from this, I'll send you a copy. I'm going to try to get it into **Ms. Magazine**. Do you read it?"

Woods - "I've read it."

Axford - "What advice would you have for women who want to get into sports?"

Woods - "If they enjoy it, do their best at it."

Axford - "Anything about endurance?"

Woods - "Well, every sport is so different."

Axford - "How is dog racing different?"

Woods - "Well, in some athletic sports, it depends on the person themselves being physically in shape. In dog mushing, you have to be in shape or else you will have sore muscles, but it isn't so much dependent on the musher alone. It depends on the dogs. You have to have good dogs to start with and you ought to have them in good shape."

Axford - "Do you give advice on breeding dogs? How do you develop good dogs?"

Woods - "They have all kinds of different dogs . . ."

Axford - "What are the best dogs in terms of racing?"

Woods - "Generally, just your Alaskan Huskie -- it's got the endurance, and the drive to run and know to pull in harness. They like to run."

Axford - "What other kinds of dogs besides Alaskan Huskies do you use?"

Woods - "Well my dad, Gerith Wright, has been breeding his own dogs and when he started out in the 30's and 40's he had a line of dogs called the 'Johnny Allen breed' named after the racer. He had Siberian huskies, and Alaskan huskies, and a little bit of Irish setter and just a little bit of wolf. Our dogs, now, they would be so minute that . . . anyway my dad calls his breed the Aurora huskies. And there are quite a few of them -- the mushers now in Alaska recognize it and quite a few of them have that breed in their team."

Axford - "What is the most thrilling thing about the race itself?"

Woods - "When you have tough competition and your team can still come out on top."

Axford - "Thank you very much for a delightful interview."